Coffee Makers

300 years of art & design

EDWARD & JOAN BRAMAH

Coffee Makers

300 years of art & design

Quiller Press

By the same author
TEA & COFFEE
A modern view of 300 years of tradition
(Hutchinson, London, 1972)

First published
in Great Britain
in 1989 by
Quiller Press Ltd
46 Lillie Rd, London SW6
ISBN 1870948 33 5

Printed in Italy

CONTENTS

ACKNOWLEDGEMENTS

The authors wish to acknowledge the invaluable help given to them by the following: The Royal Society, London; The Science Museum, London; The Imperial College of Technology, London; The Honourable Worshipful Company of Goldsmiths, London; The Institution of Civil Engineers, London; The Institution of Mechanical Engineers, London; The Royal Institution of Great Britain, London; Lloyd's of London; The National Army Museum, London; The Museum of English Rural Life, University of Reading; The Industrial Museum, Ironbridge; Sheffield City Museum; The House of Fraser Collection, University of Glasgow Archives; The American Museum in Britain, Bath; Hampshire County Museum Service, Winchester; National Museum of Wales, Cardiff; The Rumford Society, Harvard, U.S.A.; Provincial Museum of Alberta, Canada; Jacob Suchard Museum, Zurich; The Strong Museum, New York, U.S.A.; The International Coffee Organisation, London; Kenya Coffee Board, London; Ministry of Coffee and Tea Development, Ethiopia; Coffilta Coffee Services Ltd., Southampton; Autobar Food Services Group, London; The Italian Catering Centre Ltd., Bicester, Oxfordshire; Fairfax Engineering Ltd., London; Folger Coffee Company, Missouri, U.S.A.; John Conti Company, Louisville, Kentucky, U.S.A.; Riant Koffiebranderij & Theepakkerij, B.V., Holland; SAS Ltd., Belgium; Melitta-Werke Bentz & Sohn, Germany; Braunschweig & Co., Basel; G. Bezzera Coffee Machine Co., Milan; La Pavoni, Milan; Faema, Milan; Rancilio, Milan.
Major A.P.F. Napier who supplied information on the Napierian machine, and Peter Field of Colour Processing Laboratories, Southampton, who took over two hundred photographs, and also many other private individuals without whose help and encouragement this book would not have been written.

The authors wish to express their special thanks to Mr. Ambrogio Fumagalli of Milan whose knowledge and experience of espresso machines was of great assistance in writing the chapter entitled "Italian Coffee Makers and the Triumph of the Espresso Machine".

PREFACE

I had been in the coffee trade for many years before I realised that I was a collector of coffee machines.

I started my career in coffee in 1954 on the slopes of Kilimanjaro, not a thousand miles from where coffee began, and worked my way through the various aspects of the British coffee trade until I was selling coffee and designing my own coffee machine. I had also had a parallel career in tea, which is a beverage the public has always understood. Any British child can make tea. It is not, however, easy to make good coffee economically, and that is why so many people in so many countries have been willing to hand over the task to a machine.

In England, until quite recently, both ground coffee and the idea for a mechanism for making it were quite alien to a large proportion of the population. The extraordinary expansion of the British market for coffee is the result of a long campaign of publicity and the education of both the coffee trade and its potential customers during the post-war decades. One of the lessons that we in the coffee trade learnt was that the British would not be lured from their comfortable teapots to the unfamiliar mysteries of ground coffee unless they were provided with an easy method of brewing it.

Although descended from a long line of engineers, I have no engineering training, so I began by acquiring the odd machine, both contemporary and antique, and studying it. There was a bewildering selection. Like my predecessors, my intention was to design something which would take the uncertainty out of brewing coffee and do justice to all the expertise which goes into producing the packets of ground coffee. In the course of a few years I found that what had started as an accumulation had become a collection, and the whole subject of coffee making had become something of an obsession.

In spite of the wealth of information turned out by the printing press, knowledge still disappears very quickly. The basis of much of what is known today about the history of coffee and the coffee trade was collected many years ago by an American named William Ukers who published a bulky encyclopaedia in 1922 called *All About Coffee.* It has long been out of print, but as a young man I was lucky enough to find a copy because it is the starting point for everybody who has written about coffee since then. It is a monumental and somewhat chaotic record of facts and figures, dates and names, researched from sources which have largely disappeared. Without it, much of the history of the coffee trade, recent though it is, would be almost as mysterious as the Etruscan civilisation.

Coffee equipment was only on the periphery of Ukers' interest in coffee, but he was a tireless researcher and his book detailed as much as he could find out about early coffee machines. They are not always very aristocratic objects, and some of the more interesting ones are now a hundred and fifty years old. When they have lacked the intrinsic value of solid silver and porcelain, their survival has been entirely fortuitous. They have passed through many hands, and whatever was once known about them has long ceased to linger in the memory. Fortunately, however, since they are machines, the originators nearly always thought it worthwhile to protect some feature of the mechanism or design with a patent, and Ukers or his assistants must have spent many hours in the Patent Offices of Europe and America sifting through indices and resurrecting the most important models. Ukers' field-work has been so relied on by later writers that his occasional misreading or transliteration has been perpetuated in book after book to the present day, and in going over the same ground I have, with due respect to his industry, corrected him. His lists of names and dates gave me the starting point I needed, and here I must acknowledge the help which has been given me over the years by W.H. Beck, Greener & Co., Patent Agents of Chancery Lane, and in particular Peter Smart who has endured with patience and humour a barrage of enquiries which are not usually a patent agent's lot.

Patents are not only the best source of hard facts, they reveal the thinking and even the personality of the man or, as I found to my surprise, woman, behind the machine. Few people realise that the Patent Office is a treasure house where anybody can go and take down from the shelves the volumes, ranged year by year, country by country, recording the patented ideas and inventions of more than three centuries: not only the little people with their ratchets and cogs and coffee makers, but the giants with their engines and looms — the Watts and Edisons, Jacquards and Marconis, explaining in their own words in English and French, German and Italian, what it was that they were trying to do.

Patents are endlessly fascinating documents. Even the formal framework is full of interest. English patents of the 1840s granted their protection in England, Wales and the Town of Berwick-upon-Tweed and also in all Her Majesty's Colonies and Plantations abroad but not, apparently, Scotland. French patents of the same period cite legislation in and out of the revolutionary calendar and every inventor or craftsman is styled as a gentleman, or in the case of a woman, a lady. Madame Vassieux, who astonished Lyons in 1840 with her elegant glass cafetière is referred to as 'la dame Massot femme Vassieux'. Her contemporary, the delightful Rosa Galy-Cazalat of the manically inventive Galy-Cazalat family, was 'demoiselle' until 1843 when she reappears under her married name of la dame Martres. Italian inventors are described in United States patents as subjects of the King of Italy. In the specification the patentee can say exactly what he likes about his invention in an open letter, and many of them took the opportunity to say a great deal, revealing all the anxiety of a mother launching her only daughter into society. Some started with a little essay on the theory of coffee making and several explained in detail the drawbacks of competitors' machines, naming no names, of course. Some inventors turn up every few years with a new idea. As the nineteenth century progressed, a greater and greater number turned up with what was easily recognisable as an idea which was originally somebody else's.

When I started my systematic investigations I expected to find that new coffee machines would appear in increasing profusion as the nineteenth century progressed, but I discovered to my surprise that this was not so. There was a sudden cluster of inventions all over Europe between 1835 and 1850 and after that interest seemed to fall away. The Golden Age of the coffee machine was concentrated into a few years, rather like the legendary American Wild West. The reason, of course, was that after such a period of ingenuity there was little left for an inventor until the arrival of electricity.

A hundred and fifty years is a long time for a rather bulky mechanism which is no longer used to survive in a cupboard or attic, but many of these mid-nineteenth century coffee-makers were pretty specimens of craftsmanship and can still be found and, as the field for collecting becomes more diverse,

1

1 - Madame de Pompadour at home, smoking Turkish tobacco and drinking Turkish coffee. Print from a painting by C van Loo.

they are increasingly sought after. However, in the vast world of antiques even the most attractive coffee-maker seems to have inhabited a dark hole as far as information is concerned. Rather more than a kitchen utensil, but less than an *objet d'art*, the machine has been ignored while the more static coffee pots and urns have their own established market. Among the many hundreds of authoritative books on what is old or beautiful one may search in vain to identify a silver-plated Napier machine or Louis-Philippe balancing syphon with a gilded stand and hand-painted porcelain flask, let alone a coffee-making locomotive which must in its day have been a highly conspicuous toy for the rich. Museums, in particular the Jacob Suchard Museum in Zurich, are beginning to find a place for the more splendid pieces in their collections and there are undoubtedly many other examples in private hands. The comparatively recent interest in old coffee grinders has caused great numbers of these to emerge, and to a lesser extent, because there are fewer of them, coffee-makers are about to follow.

The larger, catering-size coffee-makers are a rather different case. These inevitably disappeared as they were replaced and, although they have acquired a special nostalgic interest because they were of a now-vanished style of décor, they are extremely difficult to find. It is encouraging that the coffee trade, increasingly conscious of its own history, is anxious to preserve them and there are now enthusiasts who will search the world for brass and copper-fitted espresso machines of a few decades ago. Less difficult to find are the early twentieth century electric percolators and it is possible to build up a varied collection of these.

Finally, readers will notice that there are many patent drawings in this book. Some of them explain the mechanisms of the machines which are illustrated by photographs since one of their most attractive features is that they still work. Anyone interested in steam engines and mechanical toys can spend many happy hours with a Victorian coffee machine, a few packets of coffee and a copy of the original patent, which is easily obtained, and this is also the best way of checking that all the parts are complete. Other drawings are of machines

2

2 - The legend of Kaldi, the goatherd who accidentally discovered the stimulating properties of coffee.

which may no longer exist, but as to that there is no way of telling. It is one of the purposes of this book to bring them to light.

I am, of course, aware that there are many fascinating coffee makers in parts of Europe that I have been unable to reach. There must also be a great deal of information in languages that I do not understand. Material has been left out because there was not room to include it, but often it will be simply that I just did not know. In that case I can only offer the excuse that Disraeli made to Queen Victoria when she asked him a question to which he had no answer: "Sheer ignorance, Ma'am".

Edward Bramah
Chandler's Ford
Hampshire 1989

THE ALL-CONQUERING COFFEE BEAN

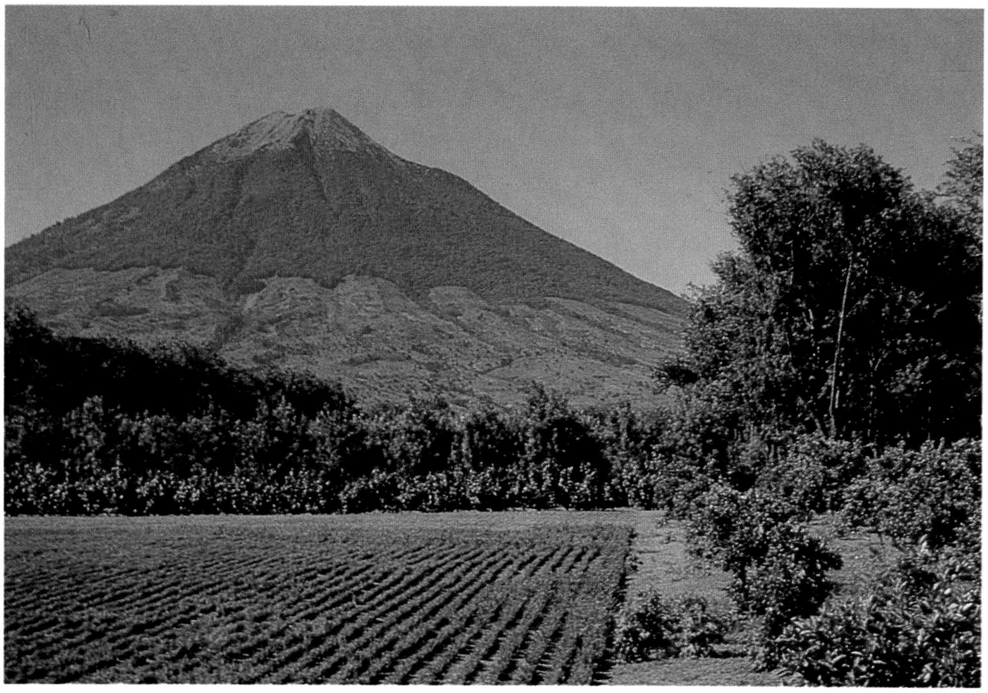

1

1 - *Coffee growing on a modern plantation in Guatemala. Anywhere in the world which has a frost free climate and volcanic soil is suitable for growing coffee. Photograph courtesy the International Coffee Organization.*

Coffee arabica is a tree-like bush about fifteen-feet tall bearing fruits which resemble cherries, and inside each ripe cherry are the two green beans which we know as coffee. Originally it grew wild in the tropical highlands on the eastern side of Africa, where animals and people identified the fruits as non-poisonous and mildly nutritious and nomadic tribes pulped and mixed them with animal fat.

By the sixth century A.D. coffee had crossed the Red Sea from Ethiopia to Yemen where it began to acquire its own legends, the best-known being the story of Kaldi, the goatherd who noticed that his goats became particularly lively after eating cherries from the coffee bush. He found they had the same effect on him, and told the monks in the local monastery who used coffee to keep them awake through their long devotions. Coffee was therefore recognised as a good thing, but no-one knew why.

During the classical period of Arabian medicine in the ninth century, physicians and alchemists systematically ground and infused every available leaf, root and berry in their search for useful medicines and confirmed that, for whatever reason, the boiled coffee bean yielded a harmless, mild stimulant. Various curative properties were claimed for it, and it spread slowly but irresistibly during the course of several centuries to Aden, Medina, Mecca and as far as Persia. In the Muslim world, where alcohol was forbidden, such a drink was popular as a help to meditation and religious exercises though not without some conscientious objections from a section of the pious who considered that the Law of the Prophet on the subject of wine should apply to all other stimulants too. However, by 1500, the drinking of coffee was so widespread that it was no longer possible to outlaw it, and the plant was being grown in the Yemen as a commercial crop to supply an established trade.

The Ottoman Empire extended its power and culture through the Balkans and along the northern coast of Africa in the sixteenth century, bringing with it the Turkish coffee house. Coffee had arrived in Constantinople from Cairo in 1517 and it progressed rapidly to Aleppo and Damascus where coffee houses with names like the Café of the Roses and the Café of the Gate of Salvation became famous. In Constantinople they were richly carpeted lounges catering for the rich, the educated and the enquiring, but there were also less luxurious cafés for the less well-off. It began to be noticed that while the coffee houses were full the mosques were almost empty, and the complaints of the religious authorities found an ally in the Grand Vizier who suspected that such places might well be hot-beds of sedition. However, they were too popular to be closed by decree, and what is not approved of can always be taxed, and this was unofficially done.

The conspicuous splendours of Suleiman the Magnificent were eyed warily by the Europeans who shared what remained to

2

2 - Coffee in flower.
Photograph courtesy the International Coffee Organization.

3

3 - Coffee in cherry.
Photograph courtesy the International Coffee Organization.

them of the Mediterranean coast. Ambassadors, merchants, explorers and adventurers all became acquainted with coffee through the ceremonial courtesies extended to them, and mention of coffee, or some word recognisably similar, flits through correspondence and writings of the time. At this period, when coffee was still inseparable from the Oriental ambience which surrounded it, it made slow progress into Europe. In some countries in the sixteenth century, people would even have found it dangerous to be seen drinking such a Muslim beverage as coffee at a time when even to be the wrong kind of Christian could be punishable by death.

The great merchant communities of Venice and Genoa imported into Italy the pleasures of the Turkish lounge, modified into their own style of coffee house, rather than the merits of the drink which had to compete in Christian countries with wine and ale. To begin with it attracted enemies. Priests in Rome wanted it banned as an infidel invention, but instead Pope Clement VIII tried it, liked it and gave it his blessing. With such distinguished endorsement it became accepted into people's homes.

French travellers first brought coffee into France and introduced it to Parisian society as a novelty in the 1650s. By 1660 it was well-established in Marseilles among merchants who traded with the Turkish Empire. It rapidly spread to apothecaries who sold it to the public and in a short time coffee beans in bales began to be imported from Egypt. The fashion was picked up by the merchants of Lyons and the great trading cities of Southern France. There was even an attempt to grow coffee near Dijon, but without success. Meanwhile coffee by the shipload was coming to Marseilles from the Levant to supply an ever-increasing demand.

In 1669 the Turkish ambassador from Mohammed IV arrived in Paris at the court of Louis XIV, bringing with him a large quantity of coffee for himself and his suite. It aroused a great deal of interest, and although Soliman Aga left after less than a year, the custom of drinking coffee remained behind and an Armenian named Pascal, believed to have once been in the service of the Turkish ambassador, did a brisk business at the St. Germain Fair in 1672 where he served coffee from a kiosk. After the fair closed, Pascal sent boys round the Latin Quarter of Paris calling "Café! Café!" and selling door-to-door from large urns which were heated by lamps or portable charcoal braziers.

Gentlemen do not make coffee, but gentlemen's servants do. So beginning in

4

the seventeenth century, a chance combination of the occasional traveller setting his Levantine servant up in business combined with the expanding consciousness of new worlds and cultures, resulted in coffee houses appearing in England and continental Europe where they soon became a vogue. Coffee houses in London became important as meeting places for men of letters and businessmen. Great financial institutions such as Lloyd's and the Stock Exchange grew from them. Edward Lloyd had provided his customers with lists of ships and so attracted a particular clientele which formed the great exchange where the world's shipping insurance is still handled. Even though it is now in the most modern of buildings, members still remember and treasure its coffee house origins. Transactions at Lloyd's take place in a huge dealing space which is still called 'the room' and the messengers are still 'waiters'.

The early English coffee houses did not serve alcohol, which limited their attractions. This rather restricted view of

5

4 - Harvesting the coffee crop in Brazil. Late 18th century lithograph by Rugendas.

5 - "Lovers of Coffee". Lithograph by L. Boilly, 1827.

what should be offered to customers was matched until quite recently by the public houses and ale houses which rarely provided coffee. Continental cafés took a broader view of what the public wanted and the result was a much more pleasant environment. In Paris, the first coffee houses were Turkish in style and appealed mostly to students and foreigners, but they were soon followed by more spacious and elegant establishments which began to be patronised by men of fashion and intellectuals who had been accustomed to the salons of Parisian Society.

Louis XIV took to coffee with great enthusiasm, and what the king did, everybody did. Louis' contribution to the history of coffee was to be far more than benign approval. In 1714 he arranged to have sent to Paris from the botanical gardens in Amsterdam a young coffee plant which had been raised on a Dutch plantation in the East Indies. The old king, then in the last year of his reign, made a personal visit to the Jardin des Plantes and spent a long time with the little tree for which a glasshouse was specially constructed. He intended that seed from it should be sent out to the French colonies and although the first attempt to establish commercial coffee plantations in Martinique failed, five years after Louis' death a French captain of infantry managed to transport across the Atlantic a healthy seedling which became the ancestor of most of the coffee now growing in Central and South America.

Meanwhile coffee had been reaching Central Europe by a different route. Western Europeans sent ships to the Levant for their coffee, the Viennese had it brought to them by the Turks themselves.

6

6 - "The Coffee Seller". Print by C Vernet of a Paris street scene. Jacob Suchard Museum, Zürich.

7 - Italian silver coffee pot in the Empire style. Collection of R. Quarenghi, Bergamo.

In 1683 Vienna was encircled by the army of Mohammed IV and desperately needed to get a message through the Turkish lines to the King of Poland, appealing for rescue. Only someone who spoke Turkish would stand a chance of success. The man who swam the Danube and successfully delivered the message was Franz Georg Kolschitsky and the siege was raised. The retreating Turks left behind them twenty-five thousand tents, ten thousand oxen, five thousand camels, a hundred thousand bushels of grain, a large quantity of gold and a great many sacks of coffee. The gold and oxen, perhaps even the camels, quickly found a home. Kolschitsky was given the coffee since he seemed to be the only man who knew what to do with it, having spent several years living among the Turks. He opened a café, the 'Blue Bottle', and although at first the Viennese refused to accept traditional Turkish coffee with its thick sediment of fine powder at the bottom of the cup, they took to it with enthusiasm when Kolschitsky strained it and added milk and honey.

The great increase in demand for coffee was creating problems in supply. Dutch missionaries and botanists were establishing plantations in Java, but most coffee was imported from the Middle East and in particular the Yemen, which was jealous of its near-monopoly. Export of seed was forbidden, and all green beans were supposed to be partly roasted before they were sold so that it was impossible for them to germinate, but either by smuggling or persistence Muslims making the pilgrimage from India to the Holy Places managed to take coffee seed back with them to Mysore where cultivation was begun

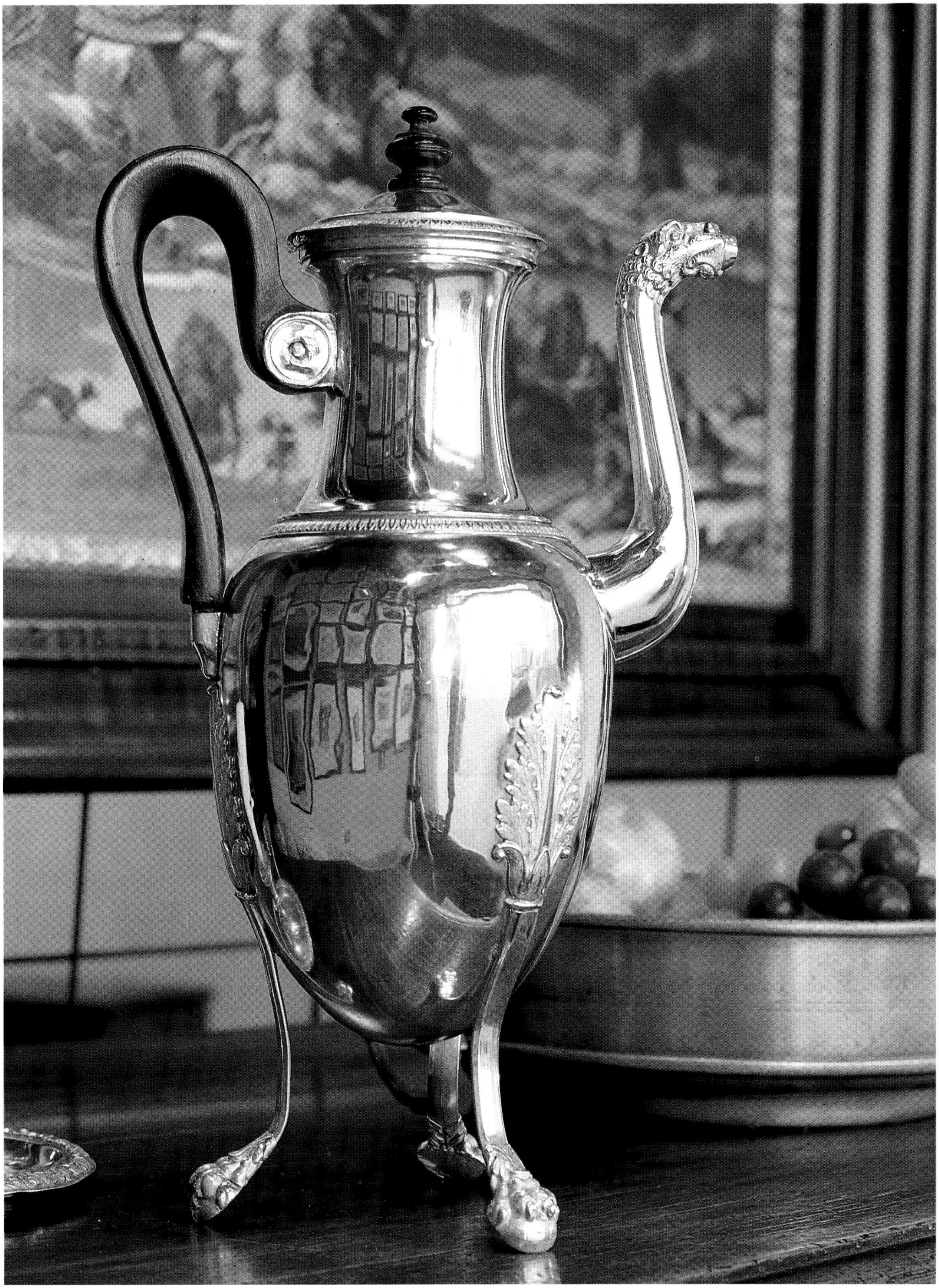

and soon grew to supply a trade of international importance. The colonisation of the Americas expanded demand which the new plantations of Brazil and Central America were created to satisfy, and during this century the East African Highlands became a major supplier of coffee to Europe.

The international coffee trade, which now supports the economies of whole nations, is second in importance only to oil. Yet there is something very strange about the success story of a very ordinary little green bean. There was no universal acceptance of how coffee should be made or what it should taste like. For the three hundred years of its history in Europe there have been a great many people who did not really like it, but they were determined to like it or at least convert it into something that they did like, and this determination has led to a profusion of coffee makers which have a history of their own.

However, before coffee can be brewed it must be roasted and ground. Coffee-grinders are now a very popular field for collectors and there are people who have hundreds and even thousands of them. Roasters are really only interesting to the coffee trade. Neither roasters nor grinders are the main subject of this book, but they have always been very important in the process of coffee making since if anything goes wrong during these two stages, the brew is doomed from the start.

Centuries ago the berries were fermented. Then there was a long period during which the berries were roasted and then boiled whole to make the liquor. Roasting coffee which was subsequently ground called for some understanding of the chemistry of the bean so that the best qualities were released but not ruined. In essence, the coffee roasting process requires a heat which is high enough to bring out the aromatic oils, some means of keeping the beans moving so that the roast is even, and the experience to know when the process has gone on long enough.

Small quantities of beans can be roasted perfectly satisfactorily in an open pan over a fire or stove, and this method has been used for centuries for domestic coffee roasting. In Italy, beans were roasted in a glass flask which was put onto hot coals. Where larger quantities were needed, such as in cafés or to be sold by druggists or grocers, the beans were rotated in a globular container on a spit

8/9 - Two large coffee roasters. Courtesy Lavazza Coffee Co., Turin.

10 - Domestic coffee roaster.

11 - Reproduction of Italian glass roaster of 1800. Courtesy Hario Ltd., Tokyo, Japan.

12 - Spherical tin-plated roaster on a spit. Nineteenth century French. Bramah Collection.

13 - Roaster with spirit burner. Early 20th century French. Faelli Collection, Parma.

8

9

10

11

12

13

over a fire. Roasting is now usually left to specialists who can blend the beans and adjust the roast to what the customer requires. The extent of the roast is a matter of personal taste and in Europe the tendency is, the further south the higher the roast. The price of coffee has also always been an important factor. A high-roasted coffee will produce more liquor but with a more bitter taste.

Complicating the issue still further is the question of additives. Coffee was always expensive and in time of war and revolution, unobtainable. Some countries suffered more than others. Britain, France and Holland had merchant fleets which brought in steady supplies. Holland and France had plantations in their own colonies. Germany, however, had no colonies and was virtually landlocked. It depended on imports from France and Holland and this cost the economies of the individual German states so much that heavy taxes were imposed. Chicory was roasted with the coffee beans to make it go further and often replaced it altogether. It had a distinctive flavour which people came to like for its own sake and even though problems of supply are long gone, coffees roasted with chicory or with fig are still extremely popular in

14

15

14 - Mortar and pestle, the oldest method of pulverising coffee to fine powder to make Turkish coffee. Powdered coffee was also used in coffee-makers where the coffee was compressed to prevent the water straining through too quickly. Faelli Collection, Parma.

15 - Nineteenth century continental coffee grinder with wooden cabinet and drawer.
Lavazza Collection, Turin.

16 - Kolschitsky in the "Blue Bottle" coffee house which he opened in Vienna in 1683. Print from the painting by Franz Schams. Collection, Julius Meinl, Vienna.

17/25 - Selection of coffee grinders from the collection of Riant Koffiebranderij & Theepakkerij B.V., Holland.

16

17

18

19

20

21

22

23

24

25

26

continental Europe. They are no longer substitutes but perfectly respectable alternatives.

Although roasting coffee domestically has largely been abandoned as impractical in modern homes, many people still prefer to grind their own roasted beans. The finest grind has the consistency of flour and used to be done with an apothecary's mortar and pestle. The more usual coffee grinder is a variation of a spice mill and the coarseness of the grounds is a matter of preference and has to suit the method of brewing. A coarse grind will make delicious coffee if freshly boiled water is poured onto it in a coffee pot and the grounds are allowed to circulate freely, but it is expensive because a greater amount of coffee is necessary. If the ground coffee is to be compacted between strainers, the grind can be finer. Nowadays, coffee can be bought roasted and ground to suit the method of brewing, but there will always be people who prefer to grind their own, and grinders identical to those illustrated here, although often collected as curiosities, are still perfectly efficient and in daily use.

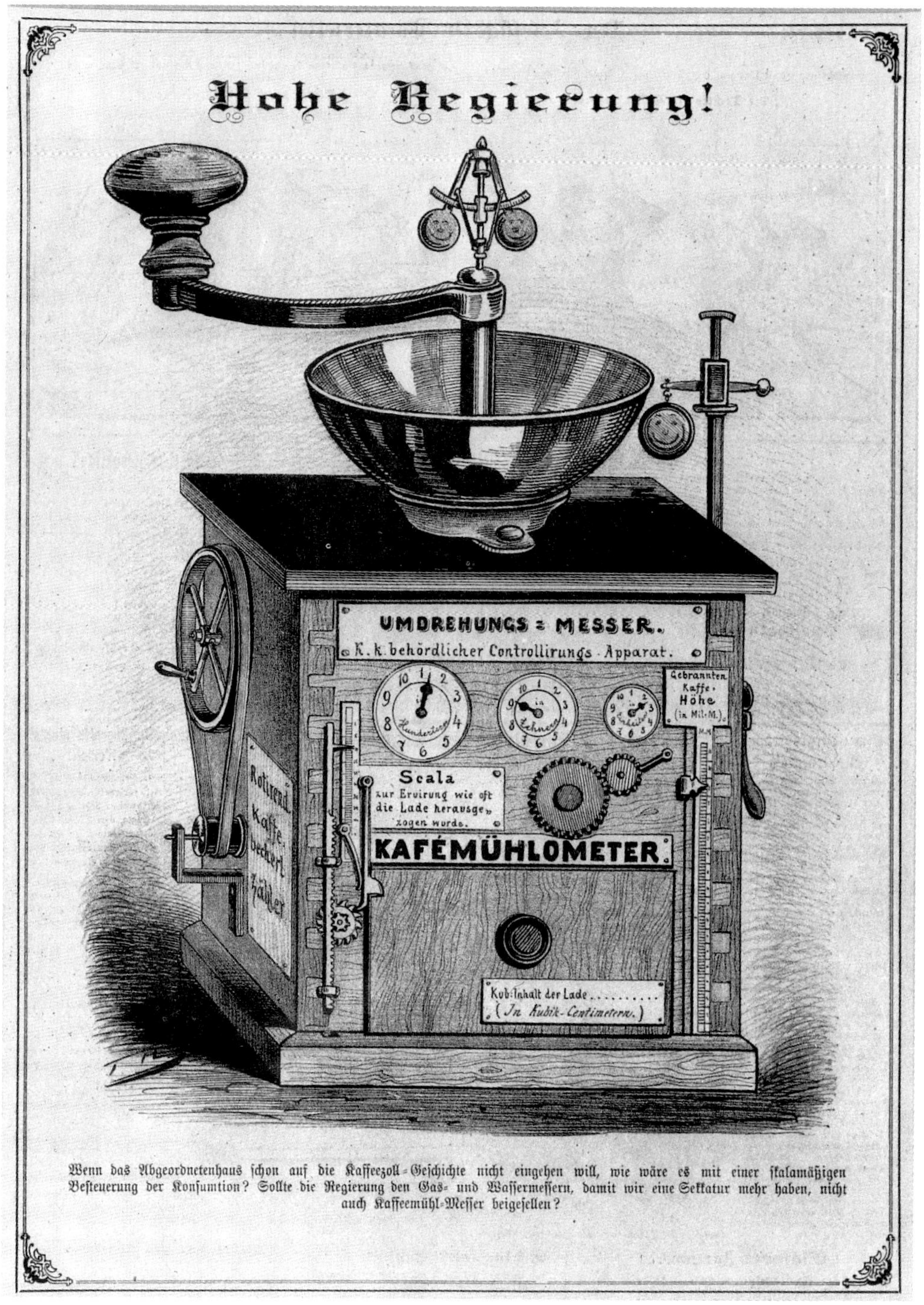

27

26 - Glass flask to store coffee. Lavazza Collection, Turin.

27 - Print of a humorous cartoon from Germany showing a coffee grinder with measuring dials. It dates from the days when the German states tried to discourage coffee drinking to reduce the cost of importing it.

ORIENTAL COFFEE MAKERS

1

The first coffee was probably made from coffee cherries complete with the bean inside and then later from the green beans alone. All the evidence suggests that beans were not roasted until some time during the thirteenth century and even then the liquor was made from boiling the whole beans. The next step was to pound the roasted beans to a powder with a mortar and pestle, throw the powder into boiling water and drink the resulting decoction, grounds and all. At this point, some time in the early part of the sixteenth century, the ibrik made its appearance.

The Turkish ibrik is a deep metal boiler with a long handle. It comes in a range of sizes and a variety of metals and is still made today by thousands of metal workers from Yugoslavia to Persia, using the same traditional designs and decoration. This makes it almost impossible to date individual examples unless there is an authenticated history or features of unusual interest. The ibrik is usually accompanied by six small, handleless cups seated in metal containers on a matching tray. It is as conventional and ageless as the European tea set.

In the desert, and indeed anywhere where there was an open fire, coffee was made by boiling water in the ibrik, adding powdered coffee and bringing the mixture back to the boil. To get maximum strength, as soon as the coffee seethed to the top, the ibrik was removed to let the liquid

1 - View of Mocha in the Yemen from a lithograph by W Giles. Jacob Suchard Museum, Zurich.

cool a little and then returned to the heat for the process to be repeated, perhaps a dozen times. Sometimes cinnamon, cloves or essence of amber were added.

This method of treating coffee does not appeal to most European tastes, but it is traditional Turkish coffee and strength is of the first importance even though it completely obliterates flavour. The ibrik narrows from the base to the rim in order that the liquor can be poured leaving the powdered sediment behind, but anyone familiar with Turkish coffee knows that this does not really work, and sediment is an invariable feature of Turkish coffee. There are people who enjoy it for itself, but it really only yields its best qualities in its own surroundings. In the countries that once belonged to the old Ottoman Empire it tastes delicious.

The ibrik never found favour in Western Europe, but the Baghdad boiler, the other classic eastern coffee maker which is much more familiar, had a great influence on the style of European coffee pots and was extensively copied in silver and ceramics.

By the middle of the seventeenth century the Baghdad boiler had acquired a

2

3

4

5

2 - The Baghdad boiler which was put onto hot ashes to boil the coffee powder and water together. Bramah Collection.

3 - Itinerant coffee seller in Smyrna in about 1820. Lithograph by B. Tatikian. Jacob Suchard Museum, Zürich.

4 - Turkish open-topped coffee boiler known as an ibrik and used from the 16th century to the present day. Usually in a set with handleless cups. Bramah Collection.

5 - Coffee seller in the streets of Paris in about 1700. Coloured copper engraving by Gérard Jean Baptiste Scotin. Jacob Suchard Museum, Zürich.

lid, a curved handle and a characteristic beaklike spout. By trial and error and natural evolution it had been discovered that the bulbous base retained at least a proportion of the coffee grounds, the extended beak was ideal for pouring and the boiler not only had a lid but also a hinged flap which covered the pouring spout, retaining the heat. Before the coffee was served, the boiler was wrapped in a wet cloth which cleared the liquor and induced some of the grounds to settle. It was also customary in Mecca and some other Arabian cities to put a bunch of herbs in the spout to strain off more grounds.

The sheer number of ibriks and Baghdad boilers limits their interest, but they can set off a rug or a low table. It is extremely probable that ninety per cent of the Baghdad boilers in the Western World have never ever been used for making coffee, but as a starting point in the history of coffee making they are important.

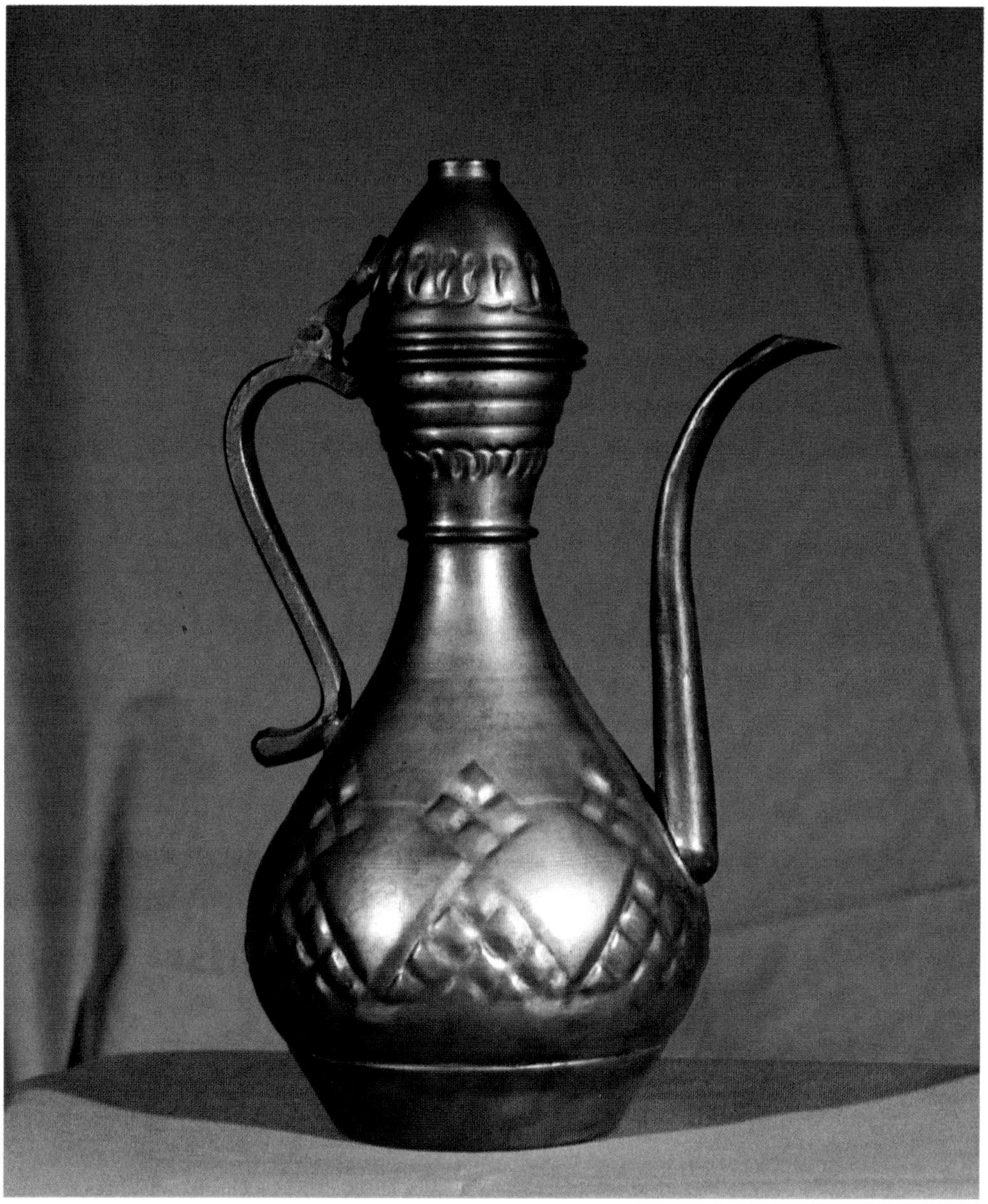

6

Although the ibrik and the Baghdad boiler have been the main means of brewing coffee, mention should be made of the ewer. This is regarded as a characteristically Persian shape and was known in Europe from the time of the Crusades as a container for wine or water. Although it did not brew coffee but merely contained it, it was the first oriental coffee pot to arrive in London in the middle of the seventeenth century. The curved spout was incorporated into the first English coffee pots and its sinuous form appeared on tokens which were used in the early English coffee houses. There was a shortage of coins at that time and coffee-house keepers issued their own, usually for a halfpenny. They were made of brass, copper or even gilded leather and were exchangeable in any local coffee-house in the same way as real money.

On the Continent, where coffee drinking did not become generally fashionable until a few years later, metalsmiths were not influenced by the ewer which remained a wine server, and coffee pots had long, straight spouts which poured better.

7

8

9

10

6 - Modern oriental coffee maker with traditional shape. Lavazza Collection, Turin.

7 - Group of Arabian and oriental style coffee pots. Bramah Collection.

8 - Arabian coffee pot. Lavazza Collection, Turin.

9 - "Jabena" and cups traditionally used in Ethiopia which has its own national coffee making ceremony. A thousand years ago, coffee grew wild in the modern province of Kaffa. Courtesy ICI Agrochemicals.

10 - Two old Turkish coffee grinders similar to spice mills. Lavazza Collection, Turin.

THE FIRST INFUSION POTS

Tea, coffee and cocoa, or chocolate, arrived in Europe at about the same time in the middle of the seventeenth century as trade expanded into new territories. Cocoa was difficult to ruin and tea proved no problem to make since it was only necessary to pour boiling water onto the tea-leaves. The Chinese made tea this way in handleless cups, but the East India Company captains sent back to Europe pots which, although they were in reality wine pots, were readily accepted as teapots. European potters copied the shapes and patterns, making teapots by the hundreds and thousands and so did silversmiths. Henceforth, all efforts to make the brewing of tea more difficult were unsuccessful.

When coffee first arrived in Europe the coffee and water were boiled together, but as the excitement of following a new fashion wore off, many people found the liquor far too bitter. In the coffee-houses, coffee was made in bulk in large containers suspended over a fire before being transferred into serving pots. Straining the grounds from the liquor helped, but matters only really improved when the infusion method made its first appearance in France around 1710. The powdered coffee was contained in a cloth bag which was suspended by a string in a large coffee maker. Boiling water was poured over it and the result was a pleasanter, milder liquor. Soon infusion had largely replaced boiling in France and in 1763 a

1

1 - A Coffee House in Restoration London. Courtesy of Lloyd's of London.

2 - Silver coffee pot by Matthäus II Bauer, Augsburg, c. 1698. Jacob Suchard Museum, Zürich.

3

4

French tinsmith named Donmartin put the bag onto a ring which fitted into the top of the pot.

This method of infusion was so similar to making tea that it remained popular in England and Holland long after it had gone out of fashion in France. Beautiful examples of early eighteenth century coffee pots have survived, some with serving taps and many standing on three feet to leave room for a heater, and they appear frequently in paintings of the period. For a considerable part of the eighteenth century, these bulbous pots seem to have been more fashionable than the tall silver coffee pots that fetch enormous prices today. Families, which a generation or two before would have been painted standing grouped round their little dog, are now shown informally sitting at table with a gleaming brass or copper coffee pot as the focus of the picture.

3/4 - Late eighteenth century Dutch coffee pots, one in brass and the other in copper. Both with three taps. Courtesy Jack Casimir Ltd.

5 - Dutch painted pewter urn, associated with the north-east provinces of Gröningen and Friesland. Eighteenth century. Height 47cms. Bramah Collection.

5

6

7

Biggins and urns developed from the early metal serving pots and these are described later, but contemporary with them was the more familiar tall coffee pot whose basic proportions have hardly changed at all in three centuries.

In the reign of Charles II, when coffee was first introduced into England, merchants brought in with them the bulbous oriental ewer with its long curved spout and narrow neck. These ewers were really intended to hold water or wine, rather than coffee, but coffee house tokens of the time sometimes feature a hand holding one of these graceful, Persian style pots. The undulating outlines beloved of orientals did not, however, appeal to the more severe taste of the European craftsmen of the time.

The earliest domestic coffee pot of English manufacture appeared in the late seventeenth century and was made of metal, the secrets of making porcelain and china being still unknown. The typical coffee pot of 1680 was in a plain lantern shape with a circular base, tapering sides and a handle at right angles to the spout. The lid was conical and attached to the handle by a hinge. A this time metal teapots, coffee pots and chocolate pots were practically

6 - Small Dutch coffee urn in brass, c. 1780. Courtesy Jack Casimir Ltd.

7 - Three copper coffee pots: large, small and miniature. Early nineteenth century. Courtesy Jack Casimir Ltd.

8 - Brass coffee pot with ivory handle and original silvering inside. French, c. 1760. Courtesy Jack Casimir Ltd.

9 - English copper coffee pot c. 1820. Bramah Collection.

10 - Mid-nineteenth century copper kettle and coffee pot from Scandinavia or North Germany. The coffee pot has three iron feet so that it could be put to stand on hot coals. Bramah Collection.

8

9

10

11

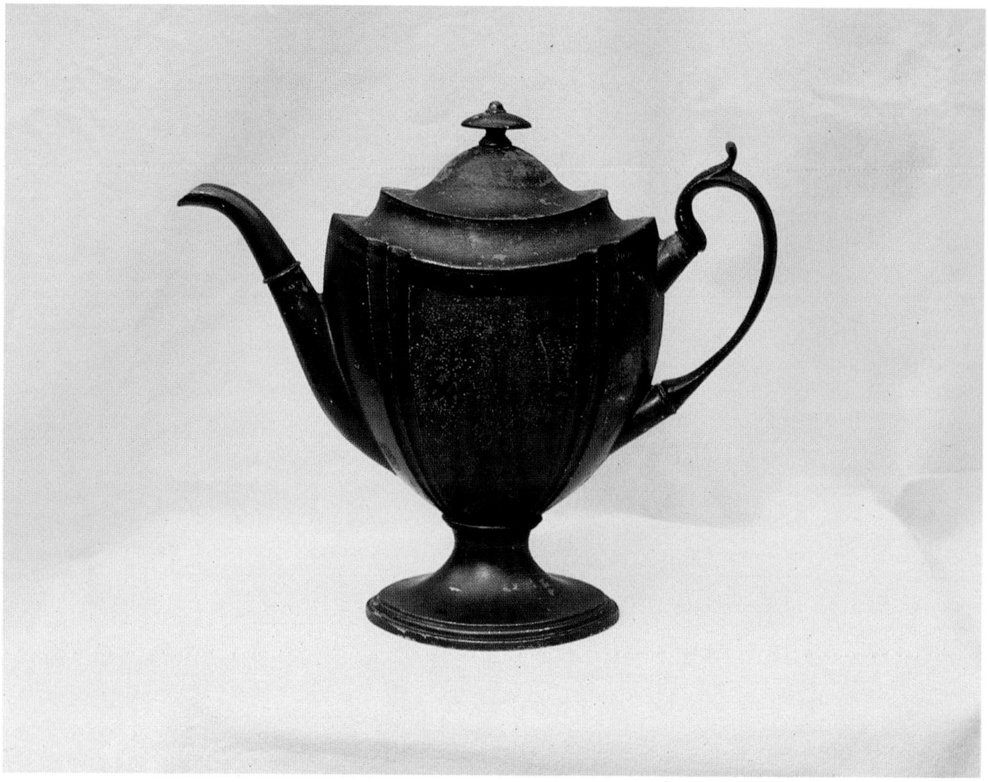

12

identical in shape, but teapots later adopted the rounder form in imitation of teapots imported from China and while chocolate pot handles remained at right angles to the spout, coffee pot handles moved round to be opposite.

By the turn of the century, the severity of this design was beginning to relax. In 1709 the straight spouts had become curved and domed lids had replaced pointed ones but the handle was still at right angles to the spout. By 1720 the silver coffee pot had reached a peak of elegance with a combination of octagonal base, straight - sided body, domed lid and superbly balanced spout and handle. The handle is now opposite the spout and the thumbpiece, which was a

13

14

16

15

11 - George II coffee pot of 1743 made in London by Henry Brind. The body has begun to be more shaped after 25 years of straight sides. The spout has shell mouldings at the base. Courtesy H Perovetz Ltd.

12 - Red japanned coffee pot with a hinge lid patented by William King. 1799. National Museum of Wales, Cardiff.

13 - Three Britannia metal pots from the mid-nineteenth century. They would have had a bag suspended inside to hold the ground coffee. Britannia metal was known as the poor man's pewter and had no lead in it.
The pot on the left was made by James Dixon & Son. Height 27cms. Centre: Pot made by Shaw and Fisher of Sheffield.

Height 29 cms.
Right: Pot made by E. Stacey & Son, Sheffield. The bone rings in the handle create a barrier to the heat and provide a cool section for the hand. The cherry sprig on the lid, the faceted spout and ornate feet are typical of the period. Height 25cms. Bramah Collection.

14 - Magnificent silver coffee pot of 1704 by Benjamin Pyne. The photograph shows the patina created by centuries of careful polishing. Nowadays, silver of this importance is only handled with cotton gloves. The Worshipful Company of Goldsmiths, London.

15 - Pontypool japanned coffee pot from the late eighteenth century. National Museum of Wales, Cardiff.

16 - Silver coffee pot by Henry Chawner in the neo-classical design of 1796. The Worshipful Company of Goldsmiths, London.

feature of the earlier handle, has disappeared.

Silver coffee pots are for collectors of silver rather than collectors of coffee makers. The examples shown are mostly English but there are many Scandinavian and American pots of great interest. Old French and Russian silver is much rarer because a great deal of it disappeared during the revolutions in their respective

17

17 - George III English coffee pot in the rococo style of 1764 made in London by Daniel Smith and Robert Sharp. The spout is an integral part of the design and the shape is similar to the Turkish ewer with a definite foot. Courtesy H Perovetz Ltd., London.

18 - Christmas at the family of the Emperor. Water-colour by the Archduchess Maria Christine.

19/22 - Coffee-pot by Johann Georg Klosse, Augsburg, 1755-1757 - Coffee-pot by Jean Baptiste Leroux, Lille, 1764 - Pair of coffee-pots by Georg Justus Hurlebusch, Hameln, about 1750 - Coffee-pot by Charles Donze, Paris, 1757.
Jacob Suchard Museum, Zürich.

18

19

20

21

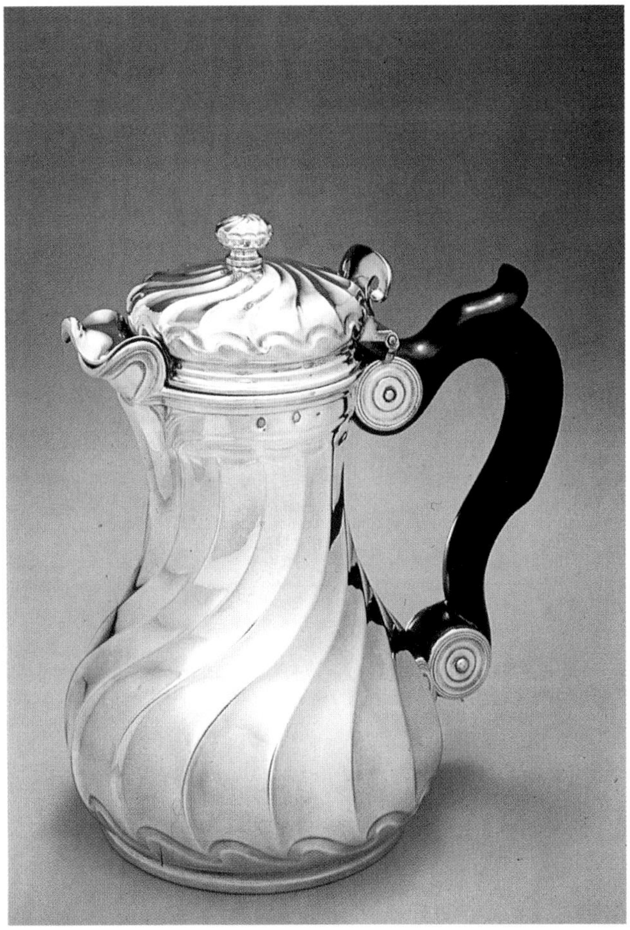

22

23 - Lloyd's Coffee House in 1798. Courtesy of Lloyd's of London.

24 - Coffee- and Teaset, manufactured by Koch & Bergfeld, Bremen, 1901.
Jacob Suchard Museum, Zürich.

23

24

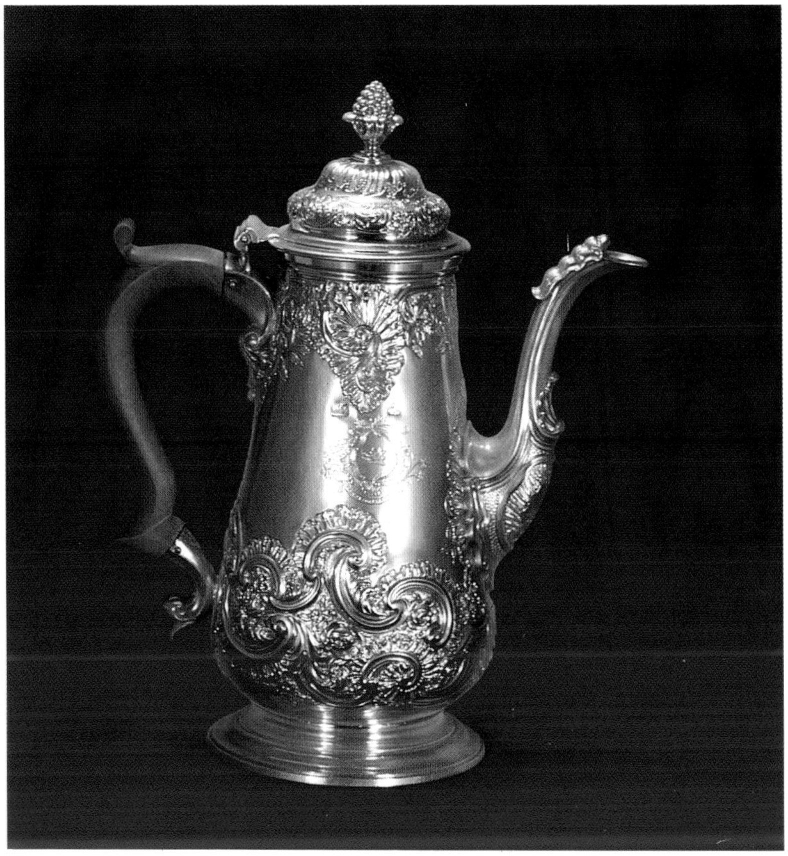

25

26

countries. Solid silver coffee-pots are a subject, and indeed a whole world, of their own. They were only ever accessible to people who had a great deal of everything else, but they added enormously to the attractiveness of coffee drinking for the rich, and for the less rich there have always been various forms of plate which closely followed the same designs.

In fact they did little to assist the actual making of coffee. They were merely containers in which the coffee could be brewed by infusion, like tea, or into which the coffee was strained for serving. This was not true, however, of ceramic pots which really did help to introduce coffee to a wider public.

25 - George II silver coffee pot of 1751 with rococo moulded decoration and wooden handle. Made by George Methuen. The Worshipful Company of Goldsmiths, London.

26 - Early Sheffield plate coffee pot of 1760. The process of fusing a sheet of silver onto copper and then rolling it ceased in about 1850 when it was replaced by electro-plating. Good pieces in old Sheffield plate are now very expensive. Bramah Collection.

27 - Wife of a Munich burgher drinking coffee in 1820. Her silver coffee pot is similar to the one shown on the opposite page.

28 - The only known antique silver coffee pot a square base. Made in London by George Wickes in 1745 with the coat of arms of Sir Abraham Elton of Clevedon Court who was Sheriff and Mayor of Bristol in 1742. Height 18 cms Courtesy Folger Coffee Company. United States.

29 - Silver coffee pot by Robert Timbrell and Benjamin Bentley made in 1714, on a stand and spirit lamp of 1709 made by Isaac Linger. Total height 28cms. This is the earliest octagonal coffee pot with stand and burner in America. Courtesy Folger Coffee Company. United States.

27

28

29

30

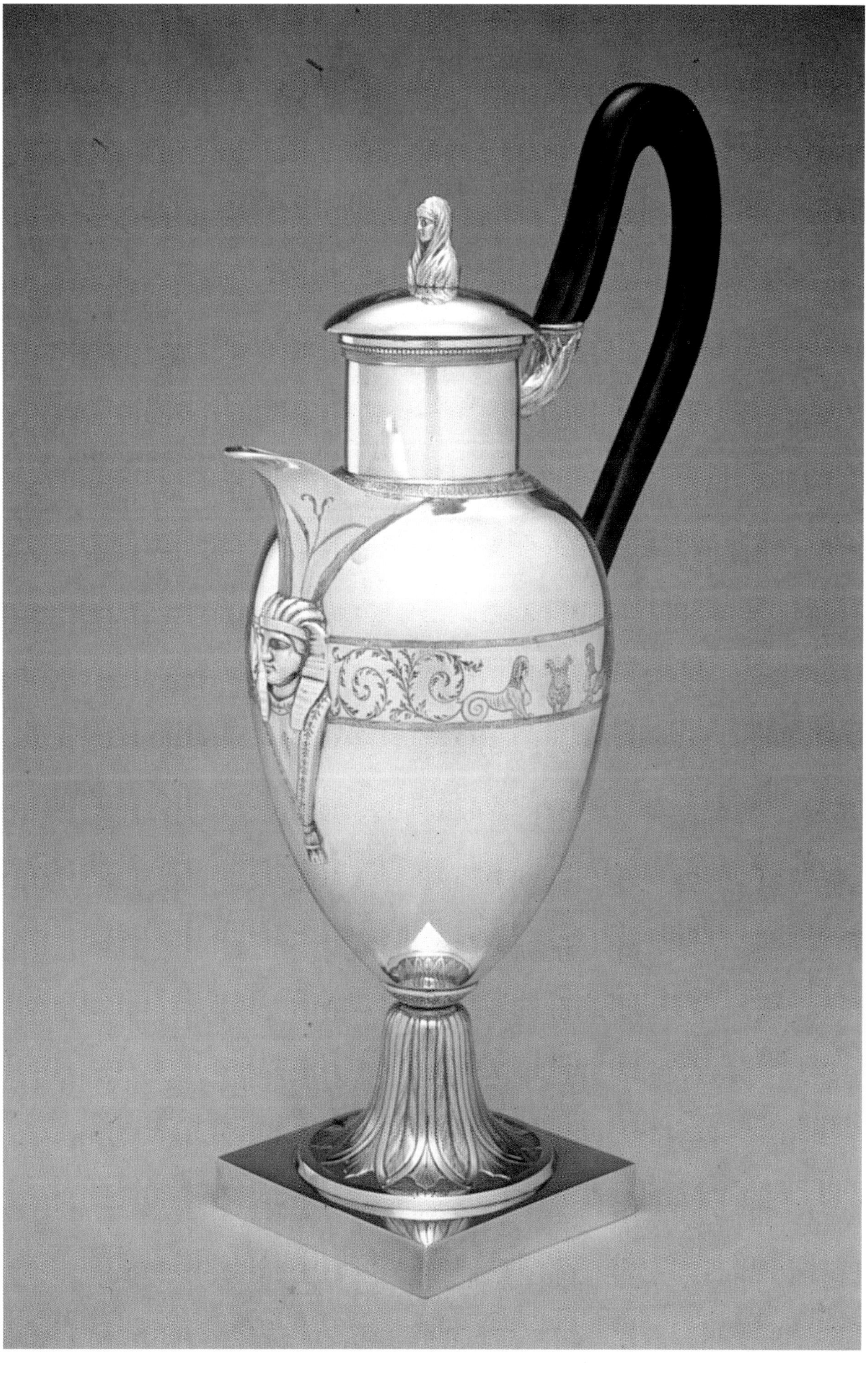

30 - Empire-style silver coffee pot by Veuve Fritz of Strasbourg, about 1804. Jacob Suchard Museum, Zürich.

THE CERAMIC COFFEE POT

1

The rapid expansion of trade, and in particular of the British and Dutch East India Companies, brought quantities of porcelain from China. The secret of this beautiful and mysterious substance was completely unknown in the West, but the determination to discover it, or at least a reasonable imitation of it, created a vast industry in ceramics which in a few years completely transformed the quality of life for ordinary people.

It is easy to forget that until the seventeenth century, plates and drinking vessels were made of wood or metal or perhaps heavy earthenware and occasionally glass. The development and rapid spread of cheap ceramics brought into millions of homes a new world of light and colour, flowers and patterns which had previously been known only to the rich. The standard of decoration on the new cheap ceramics was immediately and astonishingly high. The manufacturers took the best Chinese porcelains as their models and, as European porcelain makers in the various royal factories developed their own styles and patterns, humbler potters copied those too.

Tea and coffee owe their extraordinary increase in popularity in the eighteenth century entirely to the fact that the public had something to drink them from and brew them in. Tea presented no problem. A powerful tea trade graded the tea, exported it from China and educated the public as to what it should expect tea to taste like. The public, obediently accepting the tea trade's standards,

2

3

1 - Meissen group of Lady, Moor and Coffee-table, about 1740. Jacob Suchard Museum, Zürich.

2 - Woman Drinking Coffee by Joseph Ness, Ludwigsburg, about 1760. Jacob Suchard Museum, Zürich.

3 - Spode coffee pot with the traditional willow pattern which first appeared on Caughley blue-and-white china in the 1780s. It was not a Chinese pattern, but intended to be in the Chinese style and was adopted by most potteries, usually printed onto plates and tea services. Bramah Collection.

always remained true to the teapot. Any attempts to process tea through a machine have always been doomed to failure. There was no consensus of opinion about the qualities of coffee and no coffee trade to give any assistance. Faced on the one hand with the uncertainties of turning the green bean into a pleasant drink and on the other with the high price of coffee, it is not surprising that a lot of people began to experiment.

The first thing they found was that, unlike tea, coffee can satisfactorily be brewed in quite large quantities, and the ideal coffee makers for large quantities were the biggin and the urn.

5

6

7

4 - Ceramic Pot. Weesp 1765. Jacob Suchard Museum, Zürich.

5 - Unusual and pretty coffee grinder in ceramic. Lavazza Collection, Turin.

6 - Worcester coffee pot by Robert Hancock, transfer printed with a scene called The Milkmaids. c. 1765. Bramah Collection.

7 - Chinese pot with Imari pattern. The handle is at right angles to the spout in imitation of the earlier silver coffee pots. Bramah Collection.

8

9

10

8 - In 1837 the French took control of the fortress of Mazagran in Algeria in the Treaty of Tafna, and it is said that the troops were given coffee syrup and cold water on route marches in that part of North Africa. The "café mazagran" was served in the cafés in tall glasses but the style was copied in china and also metal. They are still made in France as souvenirs.

9 - English pearlware coffee pot with exotic bird and leaves added in sponge decoration dating from about 1790. Bramah Collection.

10 - Superb Worcester coffee pot, underglaze scale blue ground (the scales hand-painted in cobalt oxide) with reserve panels outlined with fine gilding and painted with exotic birds. c. 1770. Courtesy the Dyson Perrins Museum, Worcester.

11 - Coffee service by Giustiniani of Naples with vividly imaginative Egyptian theme. c. 1820. The art of ancient Egypt had become very fashionable when Napoleon started systematic excavations during his Egyptian campaign. Jacob Suchard Museum, Zürich.

12 - Coffee- and Tea-service, Meissen, about 1760, Jacob Suchard Museum, Zürich.

11

12

13

13 - Coffee pot with Japanese flower branches, Capodimonte, about 1745. Jacob Suchard Museum, Zürich.

14 - Staffordshire creamware coffee pot decorated with polychrome floral spray c. 1785. Bramah Collection.

15 - St. Amand Nord coffee pot. Mid-nineteenth century. Originally made by the Fauquez family in the eighteenth century and revived by J. de Bettignies of Tournay 1818-1882. Bramah Collection.

16 - Modern Sicilian coffee pot made and decorated in a characteristic local style. Lucchetti Collection, Bergamo.

14

15

16

BIGGINS

1

1 - *A mid-nineteenth century café-restaurant in Paris.*

It is believed that the biggin came into general use in about 1817 through the efforts of a Mr. Biggin, but the word could come from the Dutch 'beggelin', meaning to trickle. On the other hand 'biggin' or bagging is a dialect word in the north of England for mid-morning or mid-afternoon breaks. What is certain is that the idea for its construction came from France where Donmartin, a tinsmith of St. Benoit, put a strainer bag holding the coffee onto a ring which fitted inside a metal container. Biggins could have a perforated metal container or a cloth bag inside and they were made in both earthenware and metal.

2

2 - *"Le Café". French print from the end of the nineteenth century.*

Biggin is a very lowly-sounding word to describe what were in fact very splendid examples of the coppersmith's and silversmith's art and a great many of them have survived. They were in common use right through the Victorian era in England and Holland and occasionally developed variations on their internal construction. The Evans apparatus of about 1820 has a bag to hold the coffee suspended from a float.

3

3 - Patent drawings of Elizabeth Dakin's biggin of 1848. Left. The cloth bag holding the coffee grounds has a central screw passing into the base plate. Boiling water is poured into the bag, the screw is turned by a key and the bag is collapsed upwards, squeezing out the liquor. Right. Another version in which a solid cylinder with a perforated base replaces the bag. The coffee and boiling water are put in with the perforated diaphragm B at the lower end of the screw. As this diaphragm is wound up, the grounds rise with it and the liquor is strained into the body of the pot.
This idea turned up forty years later in the United States as the Etruscan Biggin.

4

5

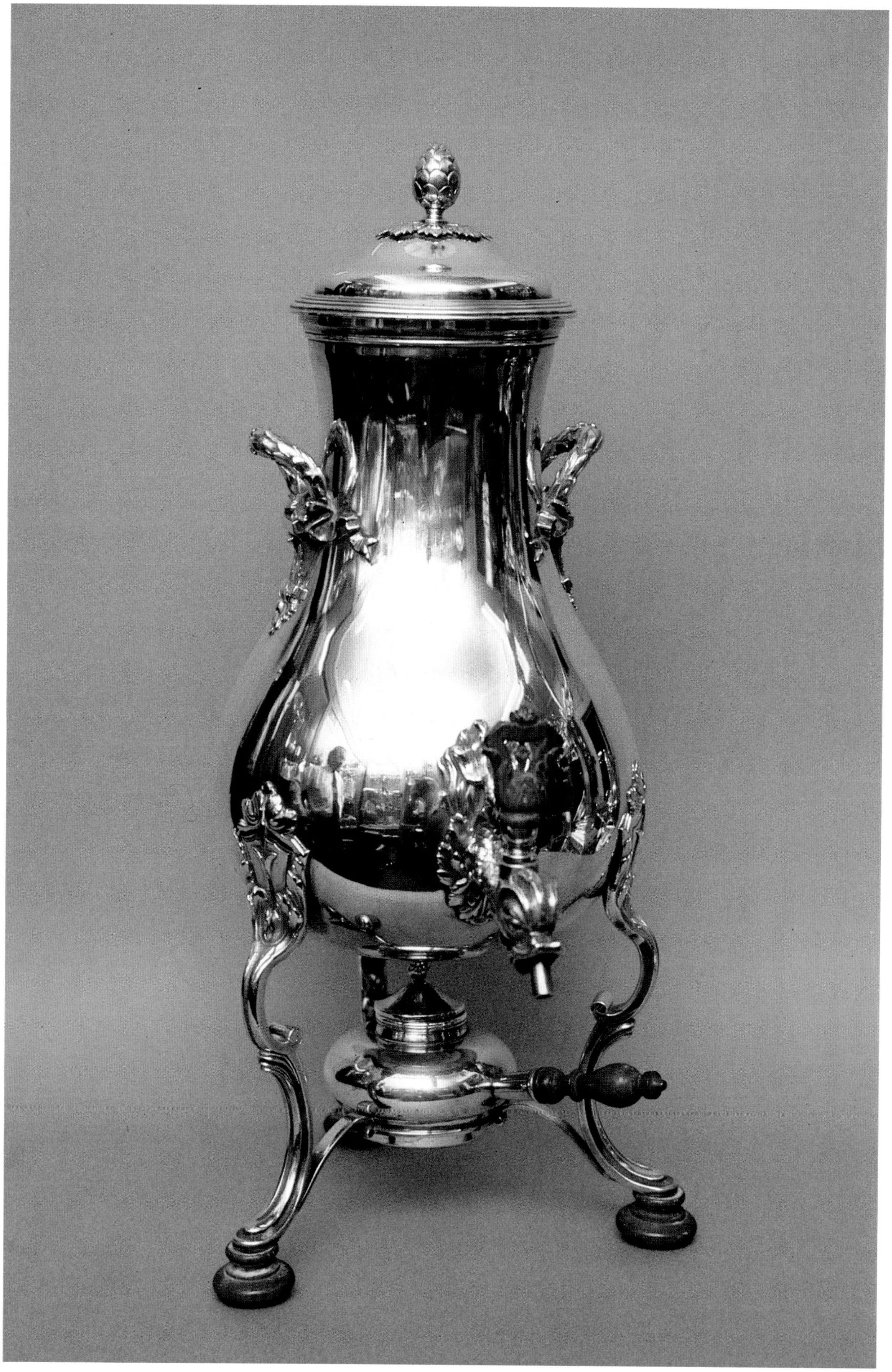

6

Biggins are not usually the subject of patents because their concept is so simple, but there is a mid-Victorian one which is interesting. William Dakin was a coffee roaster of St. Paul's Churchyard in London who applied for a patent on his roasting plant in 1847. He died before it could be processed, but it was granted in 1848 to his widow, Elizabeth, who included in it a biggin with a rammer and screw which forced the water through the grounds and the cloth into the body of the pot. Her drawing shows the typical coffee pot shape of the time.

7

8

4 - Mid-European brass coffee biggin from the middle of the eighteenth century with an infusion bag on a ring which was suspended from a ledge inside the top of the boiler. The spirit lamp was inside the detachable base which was fretted to let in the air. Overall height about 45cms. Ursula Becker Collection, Cologne.

5 - English copper biggin and strainer bag from about 1840, although the style is copied from the silver coffee pots of a century earlier. Courtesy Jack Casimir Ltd. London

6 - French silver-plated biggin c. 1860 by Bointabaret. Courtesy of R Feldman Ltd., London.

7 - William IV biggin on a stand made in London in 1832 by John S. Hunt. This is in fact a replica of an even earlier model, dating from about 1790. Courtesy H Perovetz Ltd., London.

8 - Two copper German style biggins. Both marked inside the lid Ash's kaffeekanne manufactured by the Piston Freezing Machine & Ice Company, London. Mid-nineteenth century. Bramah Collection.

URNS

Urns have been around as containers almost as long as civilisation, but were appropriated as coffee makers because they could readily be adapted. They were fitted with taps and heaters as early as the 1690s, and when they acquired an internal chimney in the eighteenth century they became cousins to the samovar.

It is only necessary to look at the 1786 patent of Lancelot Palmer to see that the urn was by no means an uninteresting and unchanging object. It was capable of infinite complexity and adapted very easily to changing styles of decoration and outer form. As a coffee-maker, it was most popular in the north of Europe and reached its peak of versatility in the Netherlands and Germany where it was manufactured by families who sometimes followed a tradition lasting for six or eight generations.

The serving pots of the early eighteenth century are really small urns, but the form benefits from sheer size since it gives greater scope to the coppersmiths and pewtersmiths. It is a very large subject and it is possible to become very absorbed in the variety of dröppelminas, dröppellieses and dröppeltrinas. The eighteenth century taps often dripped, although why Mina, Liese and Trina should have been blamed for this is a mystery.

One shape which is not immediately apparent as an urn was the tall, cylindrical

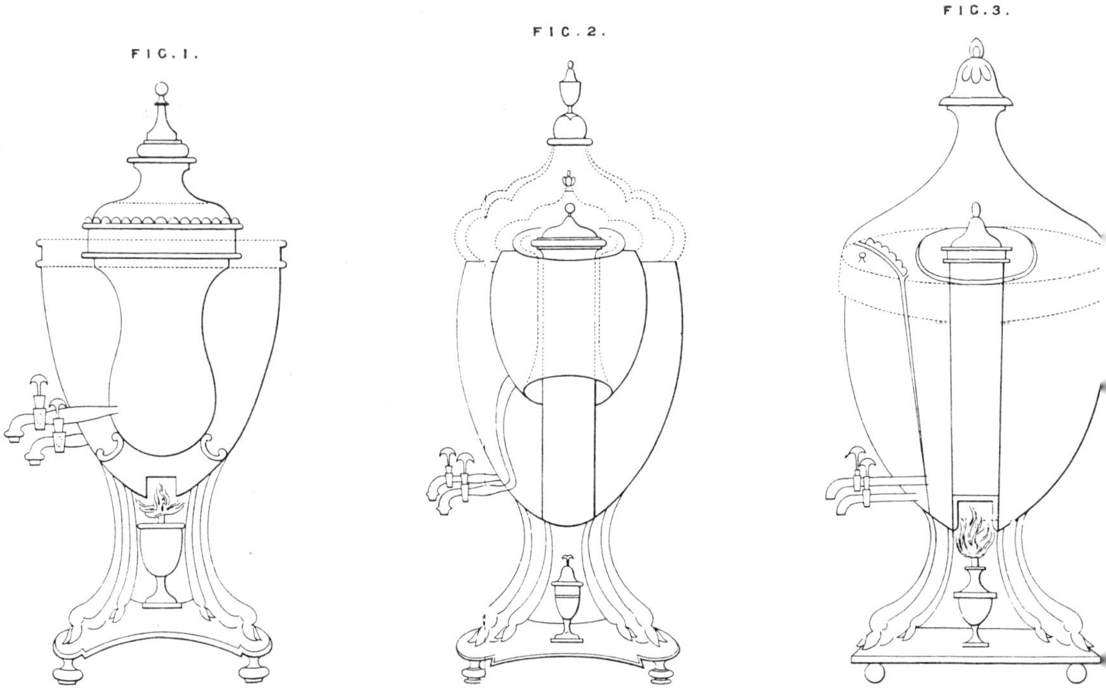

2

1

1 - Two-tier urns in Sheffield plate. c. 1800. These were made singly or grouped onto a single base when they consisted of a large hot water urn holding 6 pints and two smaller urns of 3 pints each, one for tea and one for coffee. They were used at breakfast-time in large country houses and stood on a sideboard with the chafing dishes of kedgeree and bacon. The assembled set of three urns had an overall height of 60cms. City of Sheffield Museum.

2 - Lancelot Palmer's series of drawings for his patent of 1786. They illustrate not only the way that the chimney was used to carry heat up the middle so that it acted on a considerable volume of liquid, but also the variety of different internal constructions that were possible. The water jacket in Figs. 1 and 2 was insulation for the coffee in the interior but could also be drawn off to dilute the liquor or make tea. The designs are also valuable guides to the shapes and decorative styles that were in fashion during the last quarter of the eighteenth century.

FIG. 4.

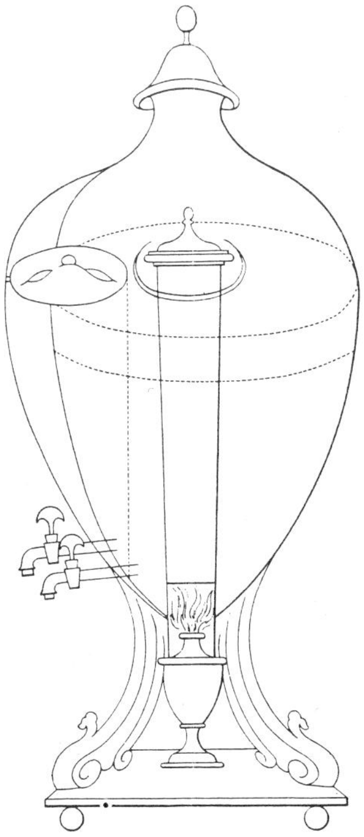

FIG. 5.

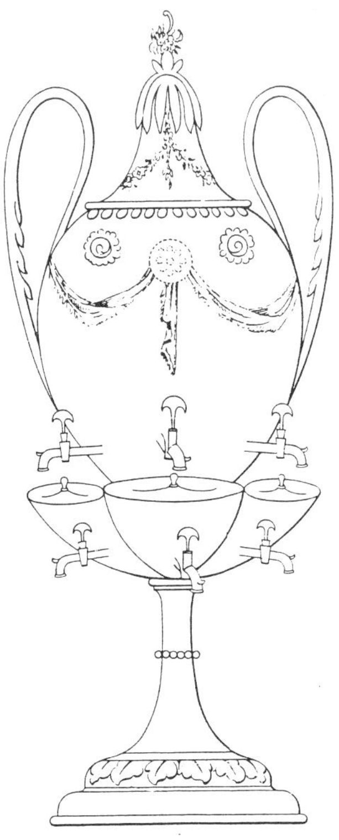

FIG. 6.

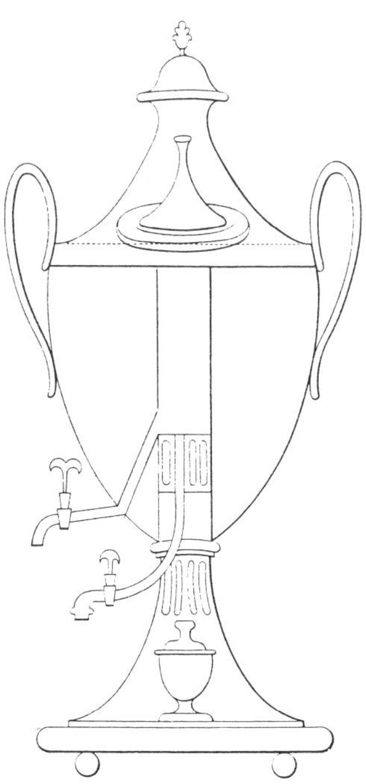

FIG. 7.

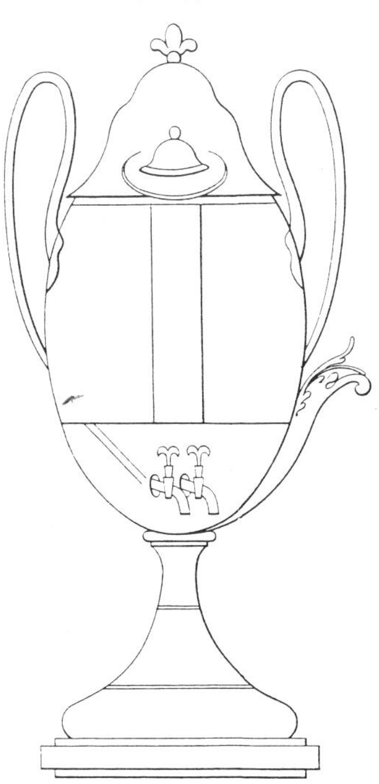

3

3 - A group of japanned urns from the late eighteenth century.
They are superb examples of the work of the Allgood family of Pontypool and the designs show the influence of the oriental lacquer-ware being imported at that time. Japanning of this quality was a slow and expensive process but easily withstood the heat from the charcoal brazier in the base of the urn.
National Museum of Wales, Cardiff.

4/5 -Two continental urns in lacquered tinplate from the early nineteenth century. The French one on the left shows the metal infuser and drawer for the hot charcoal. Bramah Collection. The one on the right is Italian from the Lavazza Collection, Turin.

4

5

boiler sitting on top of a square, fretted fire box. This was fashionable at the end of the eighteenth century and beginning of the nineteenth and was usually of tin, japanned in brilliant colours and exotic designs copied from oriental lacquer objects then being imported from China and Japan. These, particularly early ones made at Pontypool in the early days of the Allgood family, are rare, but large numbers of other urns from the period have survived. This does not mean that they are cheap. The metals from which they were made make them expensive and a collection of them would not only require a great deal of money but also a great deal of space.

6 - Single two-tier Sheffield urn of 1795 for making coffee and tea. The water fed from a tap in the revolving top into three separate infusers in the base which each had its own tap. The letter 'C' over the tap indicates the container for coffee. The other two were appropriately marked for green tea and black tea. The boiling water was kept hot by a heated metal ingot in a jacket in the upper section of the machine. This style of urn with fluted sides was known in Germany thirty years later as a 'melonenkanne'. Bramah Collection. 6

7

7 - A famous cartoon by Du Maurier. The curate, asked by the bishop about the quality of his egg, replies, "Thank you, my lord. It is excellent in parts". The large urn was a common feature of upper-class breakfast tables.

8/9 - Two nineteenth century English urns with classic shape, heated by an iron ingot in a jacket down the middle of the interior.

10 - George Sharpe's patented urn dated 1827. The intention of this improved table urn was to supply boiling water from one point and at the same time coffee from another part.

11 - Drawing of John Tucker's patented urn of 1835. The invention inserts a second vessel within the ordinary urn, into which the hot water can be added as and when required. The quantity required is registered by a float.

12 - A later urn by William Padley of Sheffield in 1877. It has an air jacket.

8

9

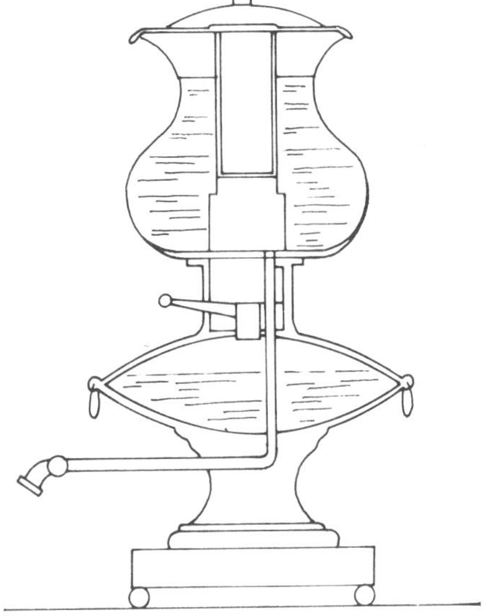

10

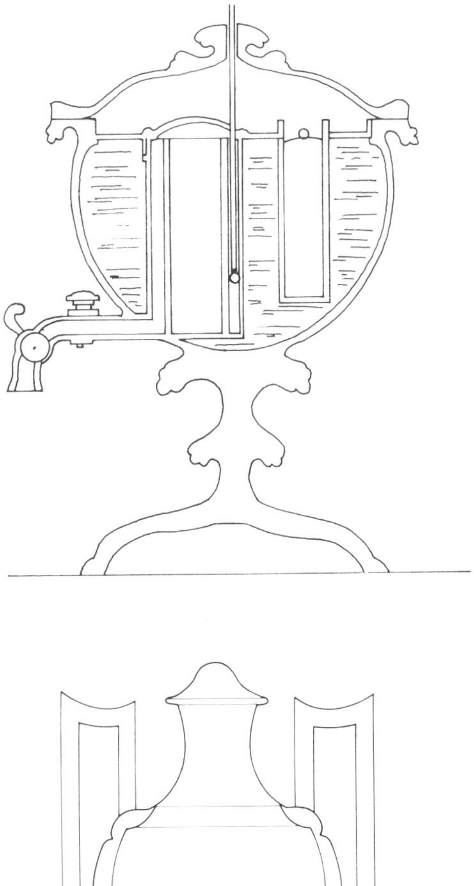

11

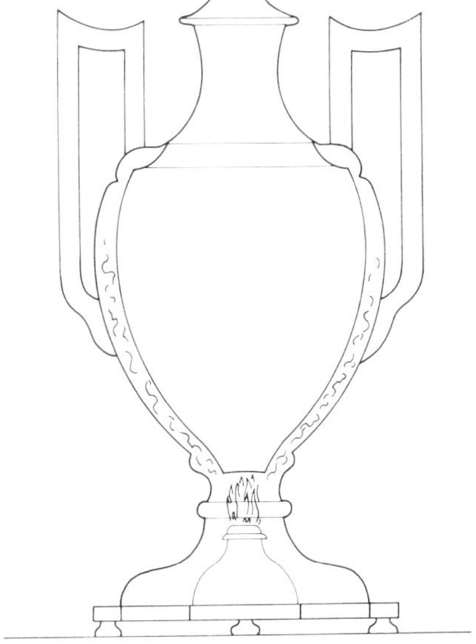

12

13

14

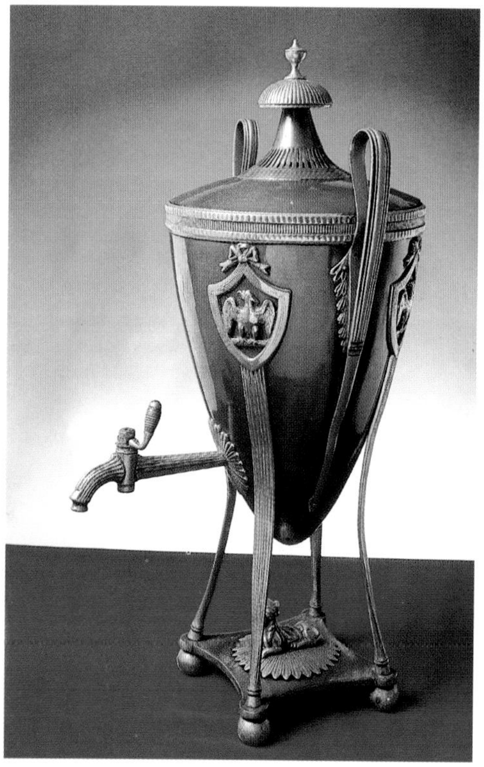

15

13 - Nineteenth century English coffee urn in electro-plate. Bramah Collection.

14 - English barrel-shaped copper urn made by John Tyler. c. 1810. Bramah Collection.

15 - Napoleon's coffee urn, found on the field of Waterloo in 1815. Courtesy of the Director, National Army Museum, London.

THE FRENCH DRIP POT

When Donmartin put a cloth bag onto a ring and fitted it into a coffee pot in 1763, he took the first step towards the creation of the French drip pot, a classic coffee-maker which has endured to the present day.

Drip pots were being made in England in Sheffield plate in 1795 but probably they were known in France before the French Revolution and the idea was brought across the Channel by French refugees. The example which is illustrated in Bradbury's 'History of Old Sheffield Plate' is quite sophisticated and has a combination teapot and two-tier coffee pot on a stand which holds a spirit heater. There is nothing experimental about it.

Jean Baptiste de Belloy, Archbishop of Paris and a renowned epicure, is usually given the credit for first popularising the drip pot and even for having designed it. He certainly gave it his name. He was born in 1709 and died in 1808 and in the course of his long life would have been able to influence a lot of people with his opinion that coffee should on no account be boiled or the flavour would be ruined. The de Belloy pot had two tiers with a strainer as the base of the upper part and a spout with a stopper in the lower

1

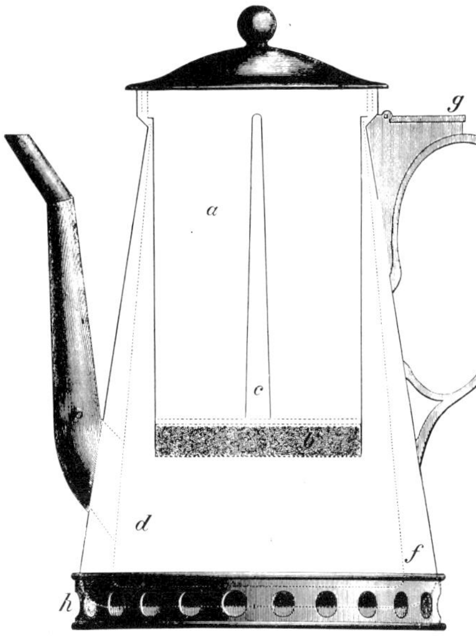

1 - Section drawing of the Rumford pot which had a double skin with a space between (f). This was filled with hot water at (g) as insulation for the coffee.

part. Coffee powder was put into the top section and pressed down hard with a rammer. This was necessary to prevent the water passing through too quickly and failing to extract all the qualities of the coffee. When boiling water was poured over it, the filtering process was delayed further by the resistance of the air trapped in the bottom by the stopper. When the powder was judged to be completely saturated, the stopper was removed and the liquor filtered slowly through the compacted coffee into the pot.

The drip pot soon became very popular in France, not only with the public but with craftsmen because it could be easily manufactured in base or precious metals or ceramics. It could be small and gold-plated or large and tin-plated. There are big metal drip pots which have been in continuous use in French farmhouses for well over a century. It could be chased, engraved and fretted and, as fashions changed, so did the exterior of the drip pot. It was ideally suited to the classic straight lines of the time of Napoleon I and in Germany fitted snugly into the Biedermeier style.

2

2 - Typical French two-tier drip pot in enamel decorated with hand-painted flowers. Mario Faelli Collection, Parma.

3 - French drip pots in metal. Left: tin-plate.
Right: copper with brass bands.
Bramah Collection.

3

The English never took to it. It had an alien look compared with the comfortable fat teapot that they were used to and the Napoleonic Wars made it look even more alien. Napoleon did for coffee drinking in England something similar to what the Boston Tea Party did for tea drinking in the United States. Among the general public, coffee became associated with the traditional enemy across the Channel and for those more internationally-minded there was always the simple silver or ceramic coffee pot. In any case, coffee was soon to be overwhelmed by the huge quantities of China tea about to be imported by the East India Company and for many years was a lost cause.

The flavour of the coffee in drip pots was excellent, but metal is an excellent conductor of heat and because of the

4

4 - Late nineteenth-century drip pot in engraved silver plate.
No maker's mark, but probably French. Bramah Collection.

5/6 - Superb drip pot on a stand with heater. Silver. Made in Munich by Weber, 1831. Courtesy Ursula Becker Collection, Cologne.

5

6

7

7 - *Early nineteenth century copper drip filter. This would originally have had a spirit heater and could have been part of a two-tier urn as shown in the Urn chapter. Bramah Collection.*

8

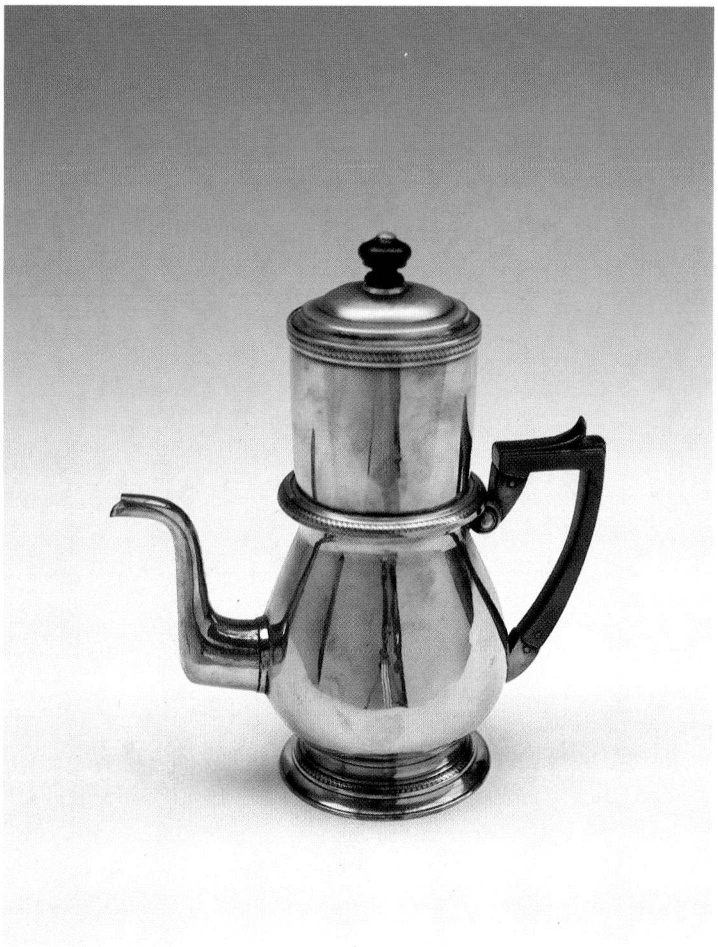

8 - *English copper drip pot, six demi-tasse capacity. The spout and handle are in the style of the 1820s which was copied from the eighteenth century. Bramah Collection.*

time taken by the filtering process, the liquor was unacceptably cool. Tin and copper drip pots could be reheated on a kitchen stove and silver ones for the dining room were fitted with feet and a spirit heater; but direct heat applied to brewed coffee spoiled it. One solution was to insulate the two containers, and in 1806 a patent was taken out by a tinsmith named Hadrot for a drip pot for "filtering coffee without boiling and bathing it in air".

French patent law dates back to 1791, the brief period of optimism before the Terror. The industrial revolution which was well advanced in England and other parts of northern Europe had barely started in France. There, enterprise not controlled by the enormously powerful state manufactories, which produced luxuries of superb quality for the rich, had been stifled by lack of capital and high taxes. Patent protection on English lines was intended to encourage French industry but it was several years before inventors felt secure enough to begin to take advantage of it.

In England at that time, the process of taking out a patent cost about £150, the equivalent of three years'

9

10

9 - Benjamin Thompson, the American adventurer and scientist better known as Count Rumford, inventor of a drip pot with a water jacket and author of an essay in 1812 on the Excellent Qualities of Coffee and the Art of Making it in the Highest Perfection. He was an influential advocate of coffee without boiling. Reproduced by kind permission of the President and Council of The Royal Society, London.

10 - "Chacun son tour". French print from the early nineteenth century.

wages for a craftsman, and in France it would have been similarly expensive. The inventors of coffee-makers in the first decades of the nineteenth century were master craftsmen owning prosperous businesses with many workmen and apprentices who could manufacture coffee-makers in sufficient quantity to show a profit quickly. They all lived in a small area of Paris just north of the Seine, surrounded by competitors and imitators (two of them had their addresses in the same building) and their patents were, in practice, a very imperfect protection. Bringing an action for patent infringement has always been a notoriously lengthy and expensive business and most patents were allowed to lapse after a couple of years. Nevertheless there must have been sufficient commercial advantage in a patent to make it worth while and it is a fact that from 1800 every coffee machine with an unusual feature can be traced back to a name, a date and a patent.

It also becomes clear that for forty years the French cafetière was very much a Parisian phenomenon and, with only a handful of exceptions, every one originated within a kilometre or so of the rue Montmartre.

The Hadrot drip pot had a double skin, a toughened metal mesh for the filter and a rammer with holes which stayed in place when the boiling water was poured in and spread it so that the powder was evenly saturated. It was a big advance, but it was improved yet again in 1809 by an eccentric American adventurer named Thompson, who was better known as Count Rumford.

11

12

Benjamin Thompson was born in Massachusetts in 1753 and after an early start as a shop assistant in Salem, began his rapid rise to international notoriety at the age of nineteen when he married, or as he ungallantly said, allowed himself to be married by, a rich widow ten years his senior. He used her money to buy the rank of major in the New Hampshire Militia but when the American Revolution started was suspected of spying for the British Colonial Government. He certainly became a Lieutenant Colonel in command of the King's American Dragoon Guards and he left both his wife and America precipitately in 1776. In London, where a confused King George III knighted him, his fertile brain turned to naval architecture, invisible ink, ballistics and the composition of gunpowder, and he probably spied for the French.

He went to Munich where by 1791 he was the most powerful man in Bavaria after the Elector Karl Theodor. His career was a mixture of scientific inquisitiveness and ruthless philanthropy and he soon made enemies. He rounded up Munich's swarm of beggars into workhouses to make uniforms and shoes for the Bavarian army. He devised a nourishing Rumford soup for the army but made the soldiers grow their own vegetables, which they resented.

To encourage the cultivation of the vegetables he created an English garden, part of which still exists, by appropriating the Elector's private deer park in the middle of Munich. The credit he claimed for this incensed the whole of Munich City Council.

He was made a Count of the Holy Roman Empire, taking the title of Count Rumford which was the original name of his wife's home town of Concord, New Hampshire, and became interested in physics, conducting a long series of experiments which genuinely contributed to the understanding of the nature and behaviour of heat. Returning to London, he founded the Royal Institution in 1800 but although this still exists, his original concept was soon changed since it was too obviously the Rumford Institution.

In 1803 he decided to settle in Paris, but since he was still a colonel in the British army and

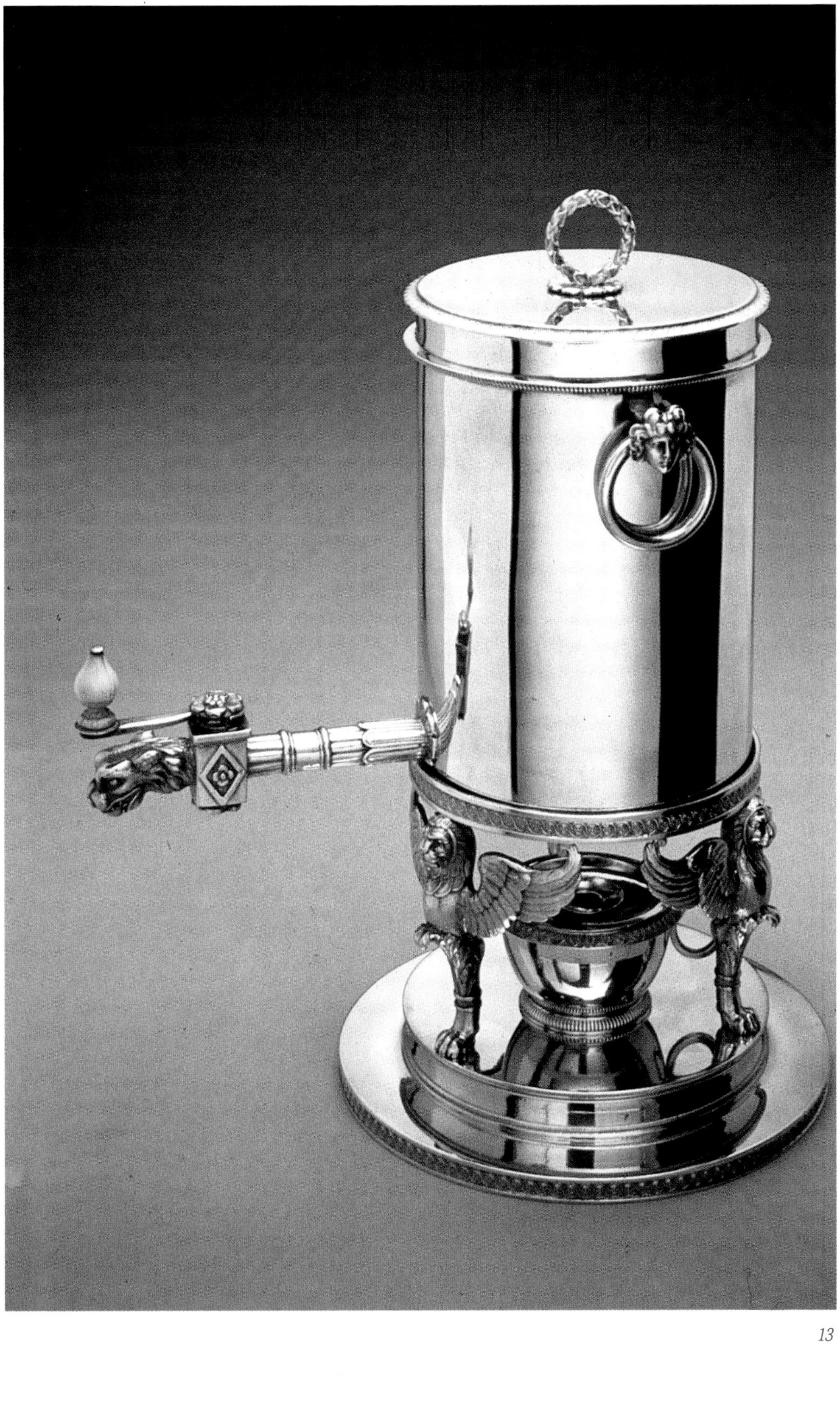

13

14

15

11/12 - Large capacity tin-plated French pot of the type which was used in French farmhouses and cafés. Bramah Collection.

13 - Magnificent silver coffee-maker by Jacob Krautauer of Vienna, 1818. Jacob Suchard Museum, Zürich.

14/15 - Two views of an electro-plated drip filter of the 1920s. In the lower illustration it is dismantled to show the coffee container, rammer and water spreader. Bramah Collection.

a mercenary and double agent of long standing, Napoleon required evidence of honourable intentions and a commitment to the interests of France. Rumford duly married the rich widow of Lavoisier, the great French chemist who had been guillotined in 1794. Never a gentleman, he described her as having been very handsome in her day and still not bad-looking. Lavoisier was a philosopher-scientist in the classical tradition of Pascal and Descartes. Count Rumford belonged to the new romantic age and was more in the style of the fictional Dr. Coppelius and Dr. Frankenstein so it is hardly surprising that the marriage was not a success.

Count Rumford's lasting achievement was to be the Rumford coffee pot which he invented in order to increase the consumption of coffee and combat intemperance among the French. In fact it became almost the only thing for which he is still remembered, and characteristically it was really a reworking of an existing concept. His work on the physics of heat and light was used and developed by greater men, but his essay called On the Excellent Qualities of Coffee shows that behind the infuriating person there was a true scientific mind.

Rumford seems to have been a systematic and competent

16 - Patent drawing of 1828 two-tier pot by Hubert-Félix Palluy, a Paris lampmaker. The spirit heater is in the space between the two sections and there is a knob next to the handle to release the water over the grounds and into the lower pot when the water boils.

17 - A type of three-tier drip pot which was popular in Germany and Austria. The spirit heater heats the water in the middle container and there is an internal chimney so that the heat can be taken up to a milk warmer. When the water boils, it is released through the coffee powder in a strainer into the bottom which becomes the coffee pot. This is the 1838 design by Koch of Frankfurt but similar ones were patented in Paris and Vienna at about the same time.

18 - 1829 patent drawing of a particularly attractive coffee maker by Alexandre Lefranc, goldsmith and jeweller of the rue Taitbout, Paris. It would have been silver or gold-plated, and its special feature is the spirit lamp on a pivot so that it remains upright when the coffee is being poured.

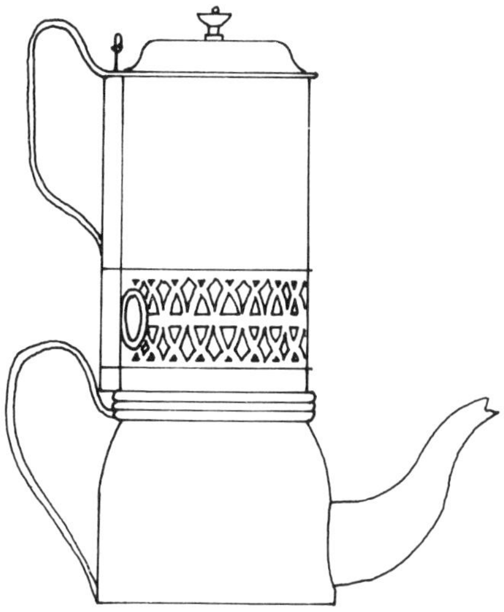

16

17

18

19

20

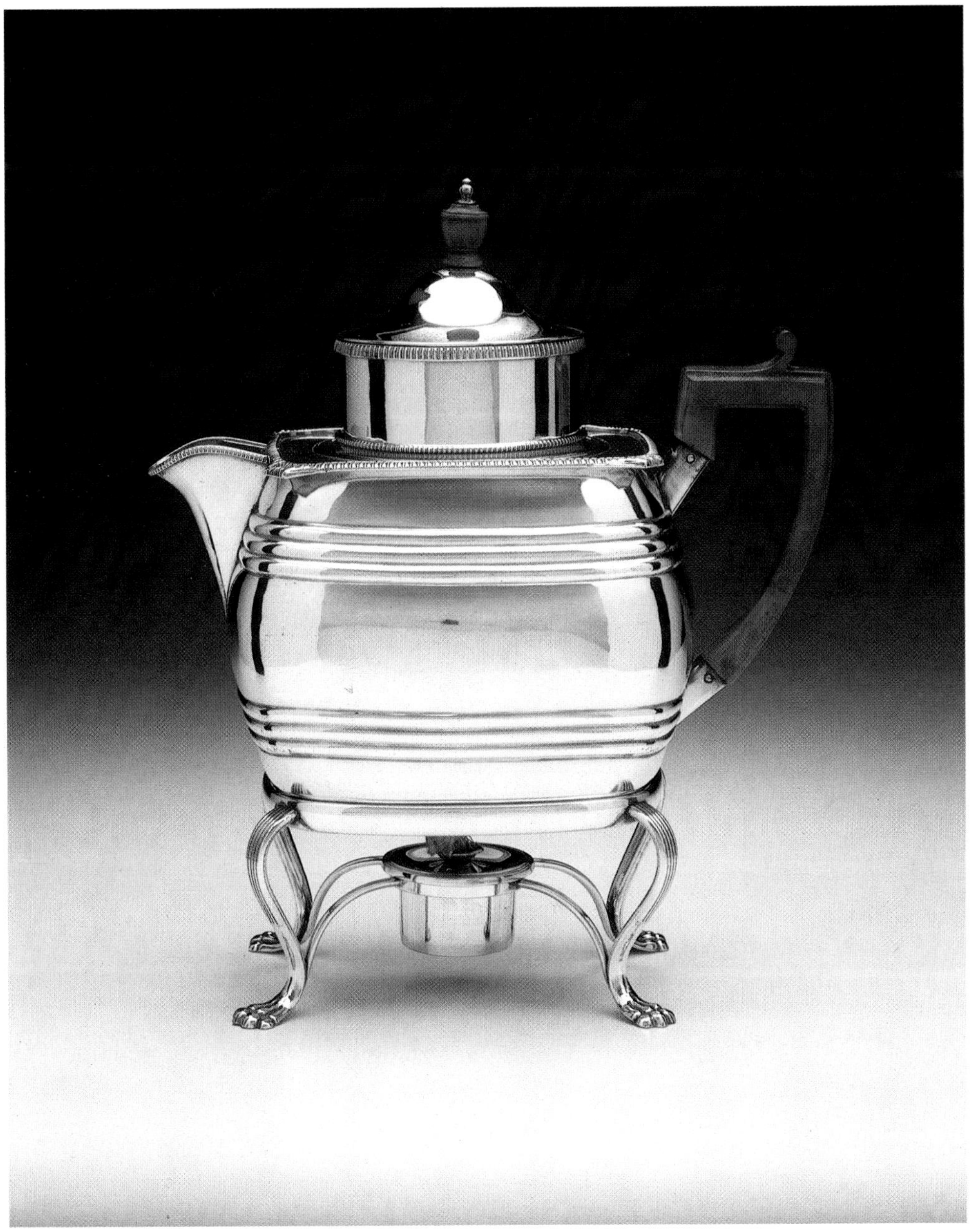

21

19 - Typical French drip pot which became known in America as the Carlsbad or Bohemian coffee pot, ideal for making small amounts of coffee. It has a strainer between the upper and lower section and a spreader plate with holes just below the rim at the top to distribute the boiling water evenly over the coffee. The strainer in these ceramic pots is usually in the form of slits. Although commonplace in continental Europe, it is rare in Britain where coffee in restaurants is usually brought to the table already strained into a coffee pot.

20 - 1930s pot with the body in the style of a hundred years previously but with 1930 handles. Nickel plate. Bramah Collection.

21 - Sheffield plate coffee maker on a stand with spirit heater and a central container acting as an infuser to hold the coffee grounds.
Early nineteenth century.
Ursula Becker Collection, Cologne.

coffee taster and his opinions are still sound today. He insisted that the water must be fresh and boiling, coffee and water should never be boiled together and the aromatic vapour rising from the brewed coffee should be returned into the liquor and not be allowed to escape. He realised that the vital essences which go to make good coffee are contained in highly volatile oils and, in his opinion, reheated coffee was the worst coffee of all.

The special feature of the basic Rumford pot was its water jacket surrounding the inner container. It was, in fact, a variation of the bain-marie which was in common use for making sauces, and there is an original example at Harvard University which houses his legacy of a considerable collection of his papers and memorabilia. He was born an American, and whatever poor opinion he had deserved in his native land, as an American he wished to be remembered after his death in 1814. Rumford's most outstanding ability was as a publicist. His ideas may not have been always his own but he still did a valuable service in bringing so much attention to them.

Although the French drip pot never successfully crossed the Channel into England where the urn was firmly established and coffee had to compete with tea, it was widely adopted in Germany and Austria where it acquired a milk heater as a third tier, sitting on top. To get the most efficient use of heat for this extended arrangement, the spirit lamp was not under the base of the pot but one 'storey' up and the water was in a boiler with a central chimney which carried heat up to the base of the milk container.

Back in Paris, Morize developed reversible versions in 1819. In its original form, the bottom section of the drip pot was the boiler and the top section was the coffee pot, attached upside down by means of bayonet fastenings. When the water boiled, the whole coffee maker was turned upside down and the water passed through the coffee powder held between two filters across the middle. The boiler and filters were detached leaving the coffee pot.

The drip pot was the connecting link between the straightforward coffee pot and the later coffee machines. A great deal had been learned and understood about the way in which heated water behaves, and the next development was to send boiling water up a tube to make coffee automatically in what was, in fact, the very first percolator.

22 - Section drawing of the de Belloy pot of about 1800 with filter basket and rammer.
Hot water was poured in with the stopper in place. The liquor was held in the top part of the pot until it was brewed and the cork was removed to allow it to strain through.

23 - Drip coffee-pot. Design by Christopher Dresser, manufactured by Heath & Middleton, London, 1886. Jacob Suchard Museum, Zürich.

22

23

24

24 - Family drinking coffee in a coffee house.
The waiter serving the customer on the left is showing great skill pouring coffee into a small cup from a pot with the handle at right angles to be spout, an arrangement not easy to control.

25 - Coffee-set. Design by Kate Harris, manufactured by Hutton & Sons, London, 1900.
Jacob Suchard Museum, Zürich.

25

THE FIRST PERCOLATORS

Filtering and percolating are really the same thing, but a percolator is generallly understood to have a different action from a filter pot. Put at its simplest, the percolator contains a hollow tube through which hot water passes and pours over the grounds. This happens because when water is heated, its volume increases and the air above it expands even more. Because it has to have somewhere to go, it goes up the tube. There are two basic kinds of percolator and their action can best be described as follows:

1. If a hollow tube is put into an open container of water which is heated from below, the hot water will rise through the tube in small amounts and out through the top. Because the container is not tightly closed, the action is gentle and continuous.

2. If a hollow tube is put into a hermetically closed container of water, the pressure of heated air pressing on the heated water will cause the whole volume of water to pass through the tube in a single action.

The inventor of the coffee percolator was a Parisian metalsmith named Laurens. It seems to have been a pumping percolator of the first type and was the first coffee machine to boil its own water. It was a considerable departure from the familiar drip pot and took several years to establish itself, and in fact the true pumping or circulating percolator did not get its turn for universal popularity until it arrived from America in the twentieth century. Meanwhile in 1820 another version by Gaudet was a sensible compromise.

In Gaudet's pot, the two filters confining the coffee are in an inner canister and each has a shord pipe extending upwards from the middle. When they are fitted together, these form a tube. Cold water is carefully poured into the bottom of the pot through this tube until the level reaches the bottom of the lower filter. When the pot is heated on a stove, the water rises up the tube and over the coffee and also saturates it from below. A stopper in the spout of the pot increases the pressure and there is mention of a filter cloth over the metal mesh to strain the powder from the liquor. This draws attention to a perennial problem with drip filters: if the coffee was finely powdered to yield a strong brew, the grains escaped through the holes in the filter and into the liquor, but if the grind was coarse enough to make the strainer effective, the coffee was weak. Until the

1

2

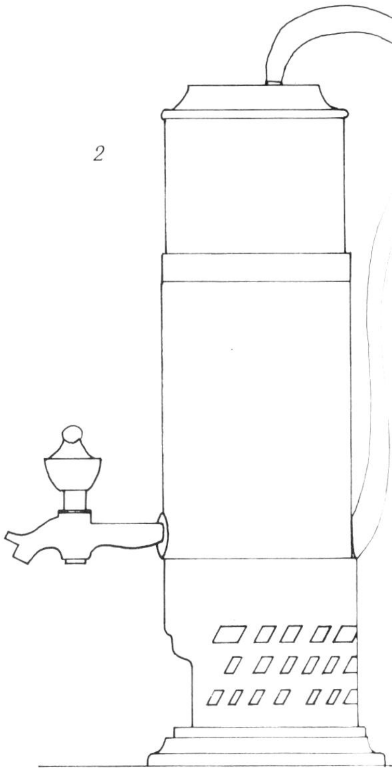

3

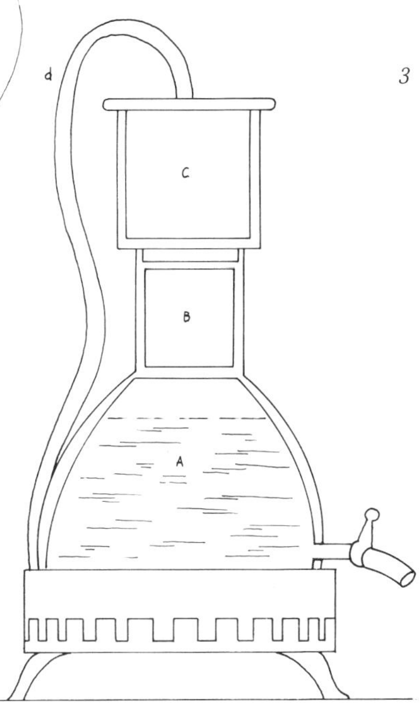

5

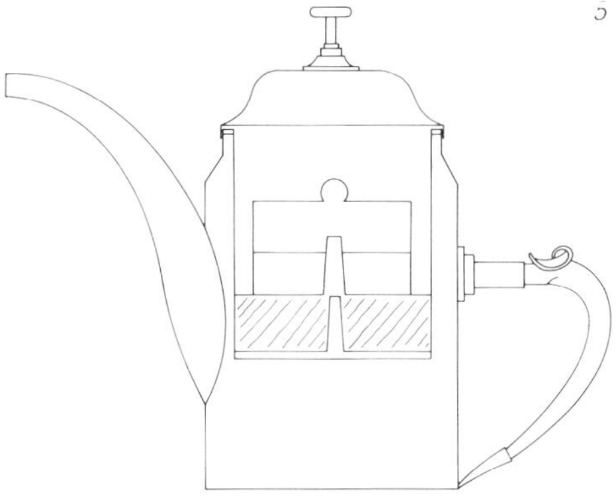

4

1 - Laurens' French percolator of 1819. This was the first coffee maker which boiled the water on a stove and drew it up a central tube.

2/3 - Two 1827 versions of a percolator with an external tube. Left: a French design. Right: an English version by Mr. Jones of the Strand.

4 - Mr. Jones' percolator in copper. Bramah Collection.

5 - Gaudet's pot of 1820 which caused the heated water to bubble up the central tubes over the coffee.

arrival of commercial filter papers, linen cloths were often used.

All the coffee vapour was returned to the pot through holes round the top of the canister. Gaudet had incorporated several improvements into his invention without alarming the customer and it produced a stronger coffee for the many who wanted a stronger liquor and were prepared to accept a certain amount of boiling to get it.

What was needed was a percolator of the second type which would boil the water and send it up and over the coffee to return it as liquor to the bottom. It was then necessary to remove the machine smartly from the heat or the process would be repeated when the liquor boiled. In 1827 Nicholas-Félix Durant, a manufacturer of Châlons-sur-Marne designed such a machine with a self-extinguishing spirit lamp, but unfortunately it was far too complex.

6

7

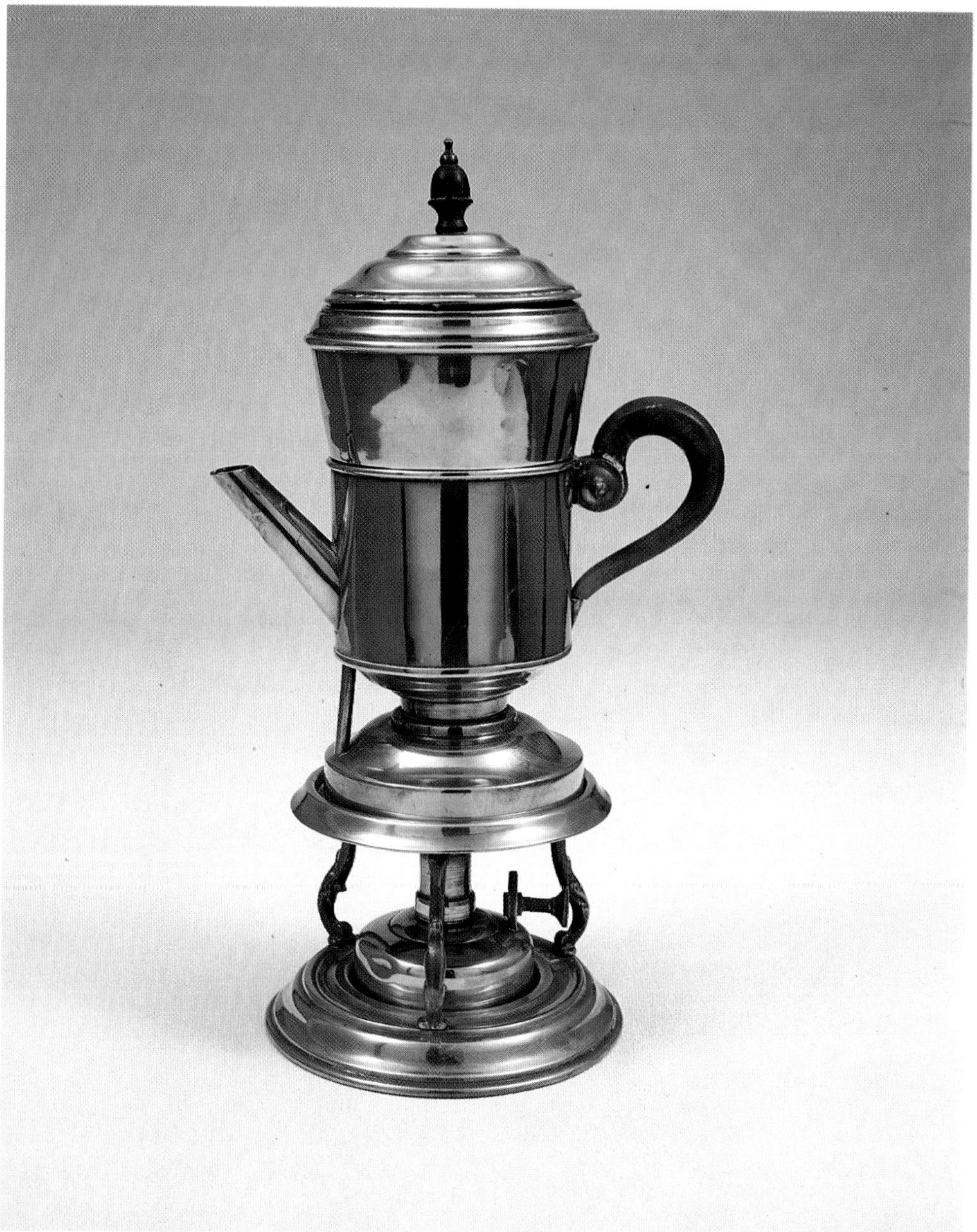

8

6/7 - Percolator in which the water passes up the handle and over the coffee. This had the advantage that the coffee container did not need its own casing tube through which the percolator tube had to pass. This was not a continuously pumping percolator. The total volume of boiling water passed up the handle all at once and the pot had to be removed from the heat quickly to prevent the base being burnt. Bramah Collection.

8 - Late nineteenth century English copper percolator with central tube. Bramah Collection.

While the English were developing engines to power the Industrial Revolution the French had become the first masters of automation. The mechanical toys and musical boxes of the eighteenth century were miracles of step-by-step mechanisms. Durant's coffee machine was very much in this tradition. The essence of the idea is that when the cycle starts, the lid of the spirit lamp is held open. When the water boils, it passes up through the tube to the top of the machine and drops of hot water activate a complicated arrangement of spring, valves, hooks and triggers which release the lid of the heater so that it springs shut. When the hot air cools, the water filters back into the boiler through the coffee. The machine shows all the signs of something which has been worked on for many years and got out of the inventor's control. As soon as he patented it, Durant realised that it was fallible at too many points and was never going to work, and he made it over to Louis-François Capy, a Parisian lamp-maker.

Capy took a firm grip on its constituent parts and turned them into a sensible machine. In his version the lid of the spirit lamp is held open by the weight of the cold water in the boiler. When the heated water passes up the tube, the empty boiler rises on springs to release the lid. This was the first completely automatic coffee machine.

Something rather simpler was being sold in London about this time by Mr. Jones of the Strand. It was a percolator in which the tube was taken outside the pot and then in again through the lid to a top container. The boiling water passes through a valve in the base of this and then through the coffee. The French patent of Jacques-Augustin Gandais also dates from 1827 and his cafetière also has a valve between the top two sections. It is impossible to say which was earlier or whether both were copied from something which already existed. The Jones percolator sold for years to the English middle classes, but Gandais is described as a manufacturer of gold plate, so his little percolator was probably very expensive.
The first generation of percolators, crafted in copper and bronze into graceful designs, was an efficient cafetière which, with care, provided coffee without boiling, but it was not the only machine on the market. For those wanting stronger coffee and with stronger nerves there were steam pressure machines.

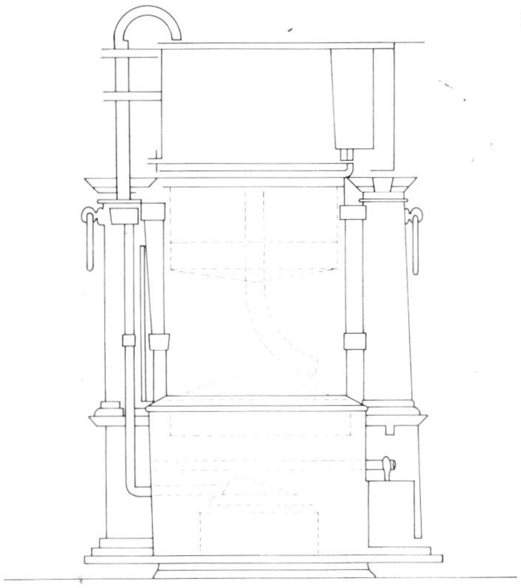

9

10

9 - Durant's over-complicated percolator of 1827 which has so many parts that he uses almost the entire alphabet to refer to them. The boiling water passed up the curved tube into the top tank, setting off a chain of events whose only purpose was to close the lid of the spirit heater.

10 - Percolator made by Laurey of Paris in 1829. The cold water is poured into the space between the outer and inner containers. When it boils it is transferred through the percolator pipe with the ram's head into the inner container and over the coffee. The boiler then becames a hot air jacket.

STEAM PRESSURE MACHINES

Percolators raised water up a tube by means of the pressure exerted by hot air and allowed it to fall over the coffee. Pressure machines which forced boiling water through the grounds by means of steam pressure originated in Germany where a prolific inventor named Dr. Romershausen brought out a series of extraction presses in the second decade of the nineteenth century. Most were large machines for processing such things as hops and sugar beet but among the range was a domestic coffee maker. In 1822 Jean Louis Rabaut patented the same design in England.

1

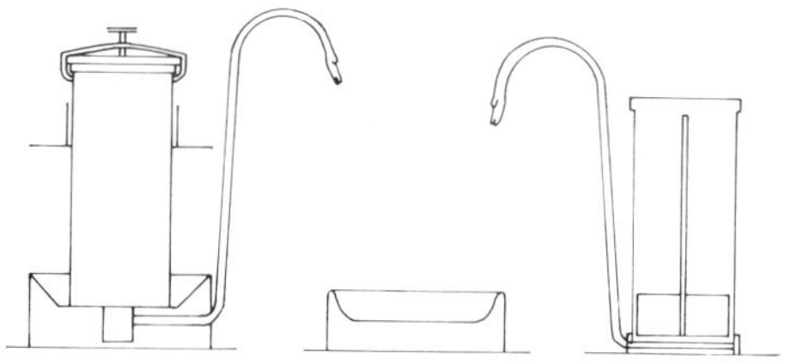

2

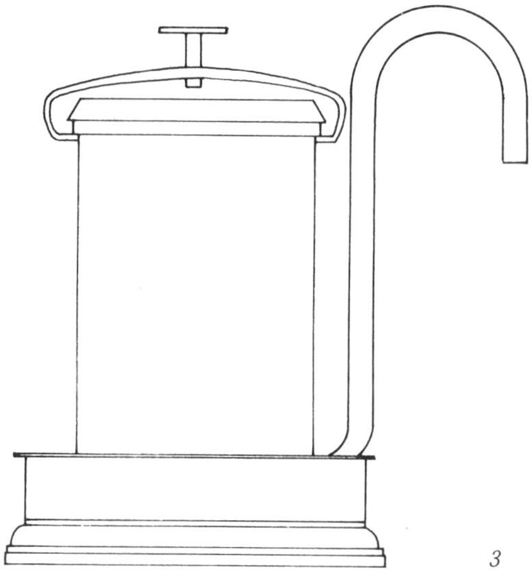

3

Several scientific journals were being launched in Europe to review new inventions and publish diagrams of them. There was the London Journal of Arts and Sciences and Repertory of Patent Inventions, and the Bulletin des Sciences Technologiques, but among the earliest was the Polytechnisches Journal by G and M Dingler, published in Stuttgart. They give an excellent idea of what was coming off the drawing boards of Europe's inventors, and at the same time they inevitably told the inventors what their rivals were doing. They also made it extremely easy for ideas to be stolen and used by manufacturers in other countries. Detailed drawings of Dr. Romershausen's extraction presses were printed in Dinglers' Journal in 1821. It seems almost certain that Rabaut copied his coffee machine from such a drawing.

1 - Lebrun pressure pot next to a coffee grinder to show its small size. Lavazza Collection.

2 - French 1838 patent drawing for the popular Lebrun coffee pot which was copied in this style in Germany, Austria and Italy. It was particularly suitable for making one or two cups of coffee.

3 - Austrian version of the Lebrun pressure pot. The heater was a bath of spirit in the saucer. To avoid cooking the coffee powder and speed up the brewing time, hot water could be added to the coffee and then brought to the boil by the flaming spirit which created downward pressure, forcing the water through the coffee and out through the spout.

4

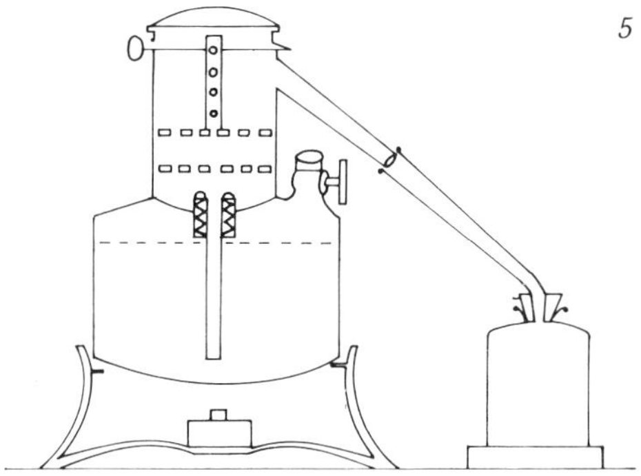

5

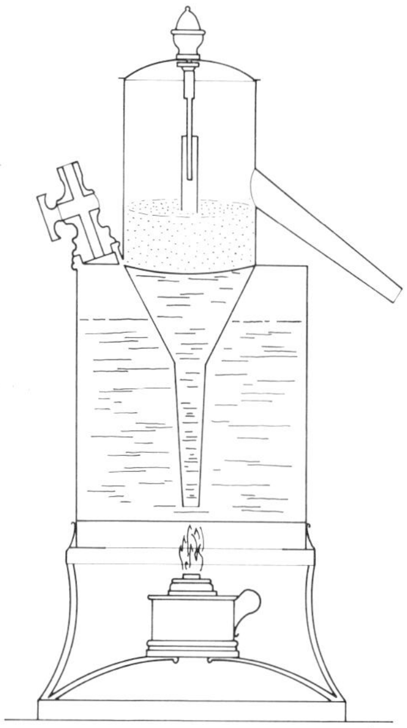

6

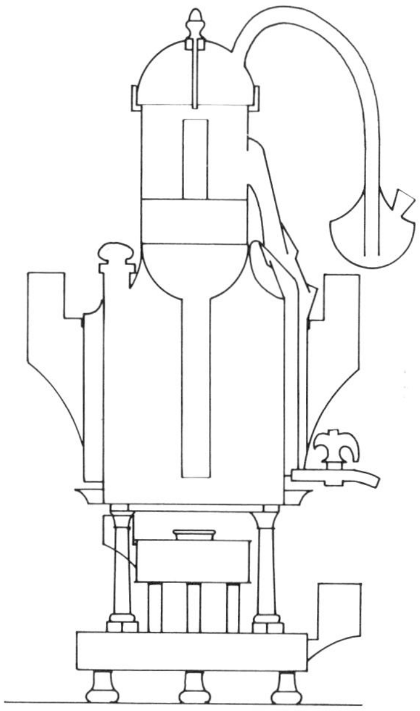

7

4 - A brass version of the Rabaut pressure coffee-maker. Bramah Collection.

5 - Design drawing of Dr. Romershausen's pressure coffee machine, one of a series of large extraction presses patented in Prussia in 1818.

6 - Rabaut's almost identical design patented in London in 1822.

7 - Caseneuve's pressure machine of 1824. This worked in the same way as Romershausen's and Rabaut's but had a tap at the end of the exit pipe to hold back the coffee liquor. The tube from the top of the machine acts as a safety valve and the small vessel of water is to prevent air getting in to mix with the precious coffee steam.

8

8 - Small, plated English pressure pot on feet to allow room for a spirit, heater. This is a late nineteenth century version of Lebrun's design. Bramah Collection.

Who Rabaut was and how he came to be reading German technical journals is something of a mystery, but he described himself as Gentleman, of Skinner Street, Snow Hill in London. He was certainly French since his English was not adequate for the process of registering a patent and a paragraph at the end of the document states that he used an interpreter named Louis Marie Dessurne to appear before the Court of Chancery, and swear the accuracy of the specification.

This machine is very powerful. Percolators which heated the water in closed containers allowed it to flow unimpeded through the exit tube. The Romershausen extraction machine required the boiling water to force its way through the coffee basket into the upper chamber and then out through the exit pipe into a coffee pot. The resulting liquor was extremely strong because another principle of physics was added: under pressure, the heat of boiling water is above 100°C so that the grounds were not only boiled but seriously over-extracted. For those who did not mind a harsh and bitter brew such machines were very economical. Very much less coffee was needed.

Operating this machine and the many pressure machines which were to follow required a great respect for steam power. The screwcock at the top of the boiler had to be loosened to put in the cold water and then tightened to make the boiler airtight and create pressure.

The heater had to be extinguished as soon as the boiling water had risen to avoid an explosive build - up of steam and even assembling the machine was a complicated procedure. The coffee powder had to be properly compacted between its two filters, the lid fitted to ensure a hermetic seal, and the safety valve checked. Anyone experimenting with a nineteenth century coffee maker will soon learn a great deal that we have forgotten about steam, in particular that timing and a delicate touch are required. The action is sudden and violent, by modern standards positively dangerous, but it was readily accepted and became tamed and adapted to many subsequent machines.

9

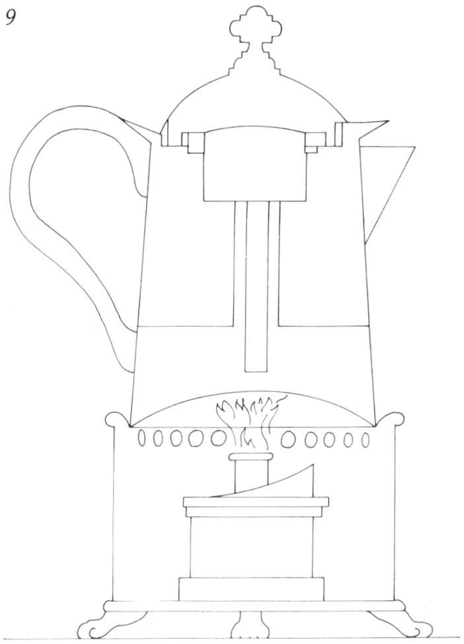

9 - Patent drawing for Samuel Parker's Steam Fountain of 1833. The boiling water is sent by steam pressure up the tube from the bottom compartment and through the container of coffee grounds with such force that the liquor hits the inside of the lid and flows back into the upper chamber. Parker's first machines were made entirely of copper or brass lined with tin, but later they were fitted with a glass lid which showed the fountain in operation.

10

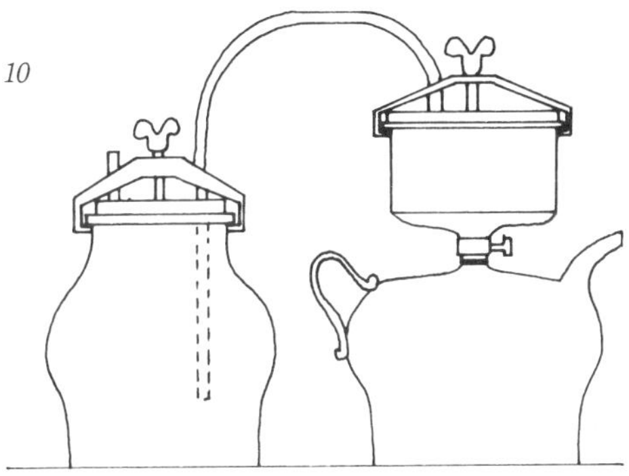

10 - One of a series of drawings by Cordier in 1844 exploring the possibilities of pressure pots. This one transfers the boiling water through the coffee grounds into a pot and has the advantage of providing a greater quantity of coffee. A more convenient version later in the century detached the coffee container completely from the pot so that any pot of suitable size could be used.

A French version by Caseneuve followed in 1824. It is the same design with a few additional features and was successful enough for the patent to be kept in operation for its full life of five years. In 1834 it appeared again in a very similar patent by Doublet and Rouen who set down in the introduction to their specification the eternal dilemma: "Numerous experiences have proved that the best manner of making coffee consists in passing boiling water through coffee powder which is very firmly compressed, but no coffee machine in use up until today has been able to achieve this because the pressure of boiling water falling on the coffee is too feeble to penetrate it properly unless compression is only slight. The solution to this presents difficulties which are not easy to solve in a way which is simple, convenient and economical." This latest coffee maker did not solve them either since the patent lapsed after three years However, pressure was not necessarily bad in itself and with a different design, the pressure machine was to have great and lasting success. The man who gave it this completely new design was Samuel Parker, a brazier with a business in Argyle Street in London

Compared with its French contemporaries, Parker's coffee machine is very English. It has its own sturdy style without being elegant, and it was certainly enduring. Examples are still to be found, not always complete inside, but with the handsome brass or copper boiler and lid and possibly the spirit lamp still in its original state. There are also many of its continental cousins.

It uses the principle of forcing boiling water upwards through a container of coffee grounds or powder, and to quote Parker's words, "I cause the whole operation, except the application of the heat, to take place within a vessel of the shape of an ordinary coffee pot instead of making extract in one vessel and causing it to flow thence into the coffee pot or some other receptacle, as is the case in Rabaut's apparatus." Since Parker was a brazier, the earliest of his machines were carried out completely in metal, including the lid to match the boiler, but later models were fitted with a glass dome and knob over the inside of which the coffee flowed as it brewed and it became known as 'Parker's Steam Fountain'. The sides were straightened and the proportions were subtly changed, but the essential Parker was around for nearly a century.

11 - A group of Steam Fountains with glass dome lids, mounted on a frame above their spirit heaters so that they can be tipped forward. Bramah Collection.

12/13 - Copper and electro-plated continental versions of the Parker design which became known as the "Vienna Incomparable". The plated one was manufactured by Richard Emmer of Vienna. These gained such a reputation for reliability and the quality of the coffee that by the 1900s they were being imported into England as a Viennese invention.

14 - Italian-made steam fountain patented in Italy with slight modifications in the 1880s. Lavazza Collection.

11

After a few years the design crossed the English Channel to the Continent, not to France, where all sorts of strange and exciting developments were about to take place, but to Germany and Austria where it was adopted and adapted. By the last half of the nineteenth century it had a hooped frame on which it hung like a bird cage, and it had evolved into the 'Vienna Incomparable' and even crossed the Atlantic to the United States where it was mentioned and recommended in several manuals of household economy and ladies' magazines. It appeared for many years in the catalogue of the Army and Navy Stores in London, imported from manufacturers in Germany in different sizes and fitted sometimes with a pouring lip and sometimes with a serving tap. It survived well into the 1900s, Parker long forgotten, and known, beyond all hope of correction, as a Vienna coffee-maker

Steam pressure downwards, rather than upwards, was used by Alexandre Lebrun of Paris in 1838 for his ingenious small coffee-maker. The coffee is confined by a rammer in a filter box in the bottom of the pot and the cold water is poured on top. The lid is a screwed down and the pot is flambéed by the spirit in the saucer. Within four minutes, coffee is automatically dispensed into a cup. The Lebrun pressure pot was popular for decades and spread to Germany, Austria and Italy where, since it was not protected, it was copied, improved and patented by local manufacturers.

The Lebrun pot with its narrow tube was capable of infinite varieties and extensions. The Cordier patent of 1844 shows some of these. Syphon tubes were now part of the standard components available to be reassembled into new inventions and were to become very important in balancing or vacuum syphons. Nevertheless, mere mechanism was ceasing, for the moment, to be of the first importance. Glass had arrived to make the cafetière a fashionable furnishing piece and designing coffee-makers was now a game that anybody could play.

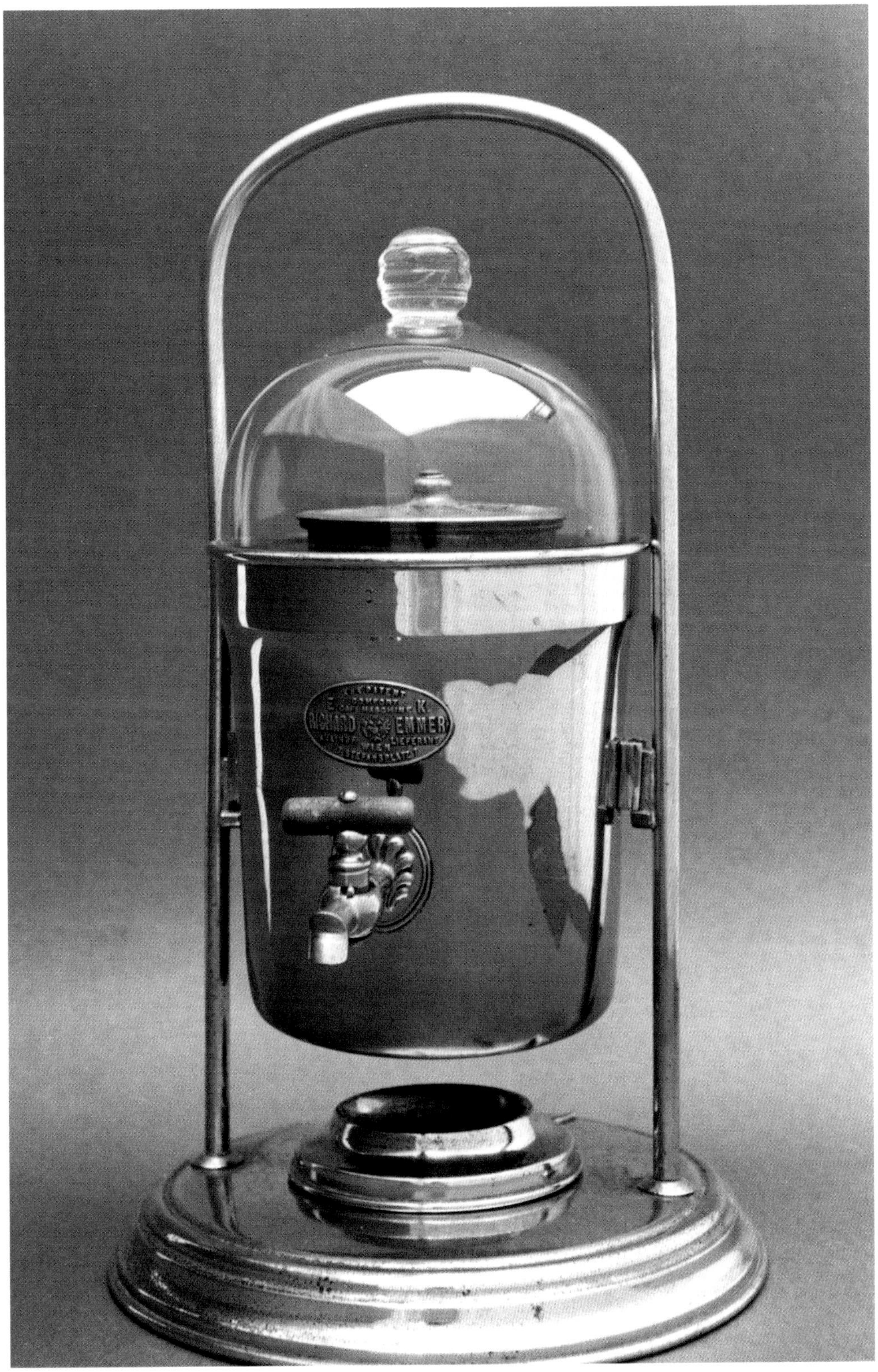

12

13

14

THE GLASS BALLOON

During the 1830s glass coffee-makers, which had been in use in Germany for some years, started to spread into the rest of Europe. It is impossible to know after such a long period at which point glass began to take over from metal, but efficient new furnaces which used coal instead of wood were turning out great quantities of pressed and blown tableware and glass became both affordable and fashionable.

The first French coffee-makers using glass had a metal boiler from which the water passed upwards into a glass retort of the type blown to withstand heat in laboratories, and they had a double action. Steam pressure made the water rise to mix with the coffee in the flask and then when the heater was removed, the air in the boiler condensed, creating a partial vacuum and the coffee liquor was drawn back through a filter.

Richard's French patent of 1838 includes a design which is entirely of glass which he admits he has copied unaltered from an inventor in Berlin. Its vase-shaped top seems to have been characteristically German and it could support a milk heater. It behaved like a percolator but its internal arrangement has an interesting feature. Instead of a straight central tube, there is an inverted funnel which gathers the heated water from almost the whole of the base of the boiler. This should be very efficient, but for some reason it was never as popular as the straight tube.

Beunat of Alsace also used a vase-shaped flask, and so did Mority Platow who manufactured a similar coffee maker in England. The Platow machine was particularly successful and was around for many years. It can still be found in both large and small sizes and although all surviving ones are copper or brass, sometimes with the vase in copper instead of glass, some of them were certainly japanned. Because the boiling water rose and mixed the coffee grounds rather than being forced through them, and the temperature was below boiling point when the liquor was strained back, the flavour was very good. It was a method which had all the merits of the pressure machine but avoided the disadvantages.

Contemporary with these coffee makers with metal boilers, an altogether more fragile apparatus employing the same principle was coming into use. In its simplest form it consisted of two glass flasks connected by a cork and with a glass tube extending down

1

1 - *The science of coffee-making being carried to absurdity. A cartoon of the middle of the nineteenth century when the fashion for glass coffee makers was at its height.*

2 - *Glass flasks were being used for making coffee in Germany during the 1830s. This is a design by Loeff of Berlin copied by Richard in a French patent. Cold water is heated in the lower part on a stove. It rises into the top compartment to mix with the loose coffee and when the apparatus is taken off the heat, filters back through the strainer into the base again.*

3 - *The first French glass coffee maker patented by Boulanger in 1835. After the water had risen and mixed with the coffee, the spirit heater was taken away and a partial vacuum formed in the boiler, drawing the liquor back but leaving the grounds in the top.*

4 - *1837 patent by Beunat of Alsace showing the German influence in the tulip flask.*

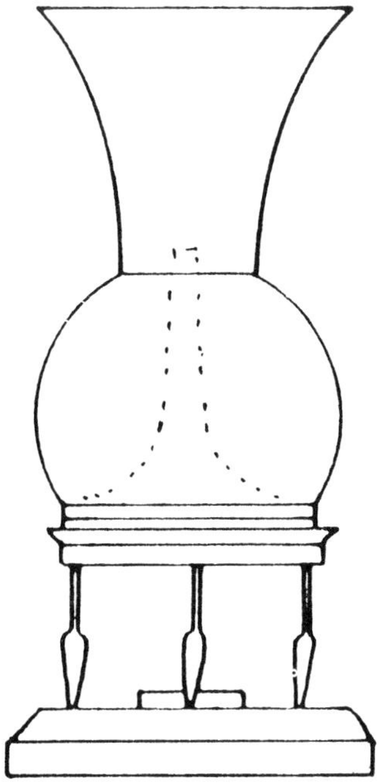

2

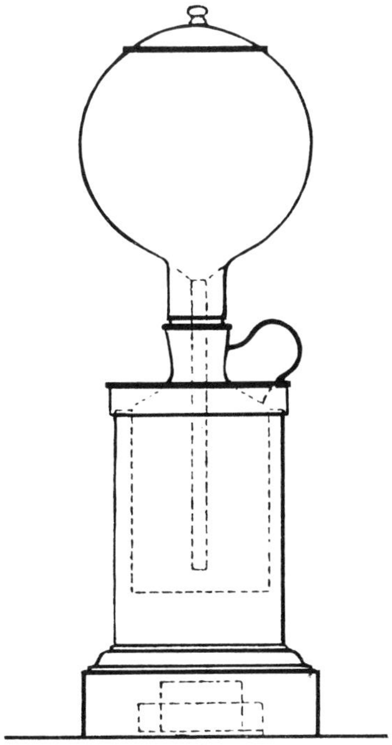

3

4

from the upper to the lower flask. It was mounted on a stand and obviously originated in a laboratory, but somehow it escaped from there into the kitchens and dining rooms of the general public and for a few years it enjoyed a huge success.

It would be easy to say that, between 1840 and 1842, French cafetière inventors took to glass as one man, except that in fact at least two of them were women. One of these was Madame Vassieux who was apparently so familiar with the double glass flask machine by 1841 that she felt confident that she could improve it. There were no details of Madame Vassieux' 1842 patent in London but it seemed worthwhile to go to some trouble to find out something about this lady, and a photocopy of her original application, obtained from Paris, proved to be a fascinating social document.

Madame Vassieux, née Marie Fanny Améline Massot, lived in Lyons so she had to go through some preliminary formalities at the local Préfecture before her specification and drawings were passed to the Ministry of Agriculture and Commerce in Paris. She was a woman of decided opinions and the clerk drafting the specification on her behalf begins: "Articles which used to be considered luxuries and mere enjoyable additions to our way of life have become necessities, and these include cafetières which each possesses its special virtue of convenience, quality of the coffee, economy, even elegance. It was reserved to Madame Vassieux to unite all these features so that the coffee may be prepared at the table by the mistress of tthe house, enhancing her reputation for excellent housekeeping and providing her guests with coffee of the best quality and exquisite flavour.

"In addition, one has seen so much business transacted, so many deals completed during the course of a meal that such a device can only contribute to clearness of mind and comfort of spirit during a long sojourn at the dinner table".

"One has only to consider the manner in which tobacco has been subjected to bans, statutes and penalties, without success, to realise that men will always insist on being surrounded by the comforts of life, and her cafetière is yet another valuable contribution."

Her design added a tap to the lower flask of a double glass machine so that the coffee could be drawn off without dismantling the apparatus, a crystal connecting stopper to replace the usual cork one, and a little coronet to decorate the lid.

5

5 - A Platow machine with the coffee brewed and held in the upper flask. A number of these machines, have survived because of their handsome, splendidly decorated copper boilers and brass fittings. Some had a copper upper flask instead of glass. This particular machine has a brass plaque above the tap with the Royal Warrant, indicating that the manufacturers supplied the royal households. Bramah Collection.

There was a Massot patent registered in the same year for an improvement to silk-spinning machinery, so it is likely that Madame Vassieux came from a family of silk manufacturers. As for her husband, dimly discernible through the clouds of cigar

6

7

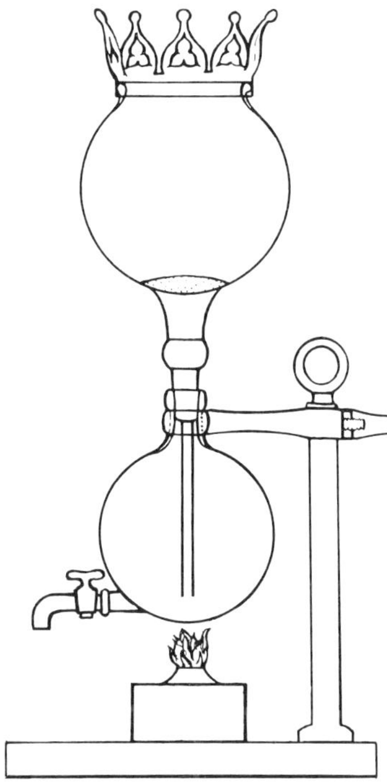

8

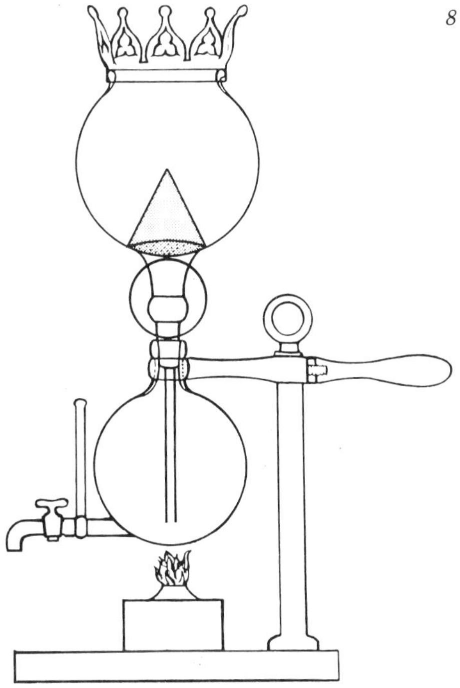

6 - *Replica of Madame Vassieux' double glass cafetière of 1841. Bramah Collection.*

7/8 - *Madame Vassieux' patent. On the left is her first design which added a tap to the bottom flask and a crystal connecting stopper instead of cork in the neck. The drawing on the right is her improvement. The filter has been altered to make a larger area for the water to pass through and there is a measuring tube fitted onto the outlet tube to the tap to show the level of water in the lower flask if this were made of metal instead of glass. The circle round the join between the two flasks marks the position of a clock face.*

9 - *Hiraux' cafetière of 1841. It was the first to have a tap from the neck of the upper flask.*

smoke far away at the other end of his dinner table between a double line of white shirt fronts, probably his business was glass.

Three days after her patent was granted on 24th January 1842, Madame Vassieux was back at the Préfecture with improvements. The lower flask was often made of metal and the spirit lamp had to be removed as soon as the water had passed up out of it or the heat would shatter the neck of the upper glass flask. It would be helpful to have some device which would show how much water was left in the bottom flask so she added a hollow glass tube rising from the outlet pipe.

As the water rose into the upper flask, so the level in the bottom flask fell and so did the

9

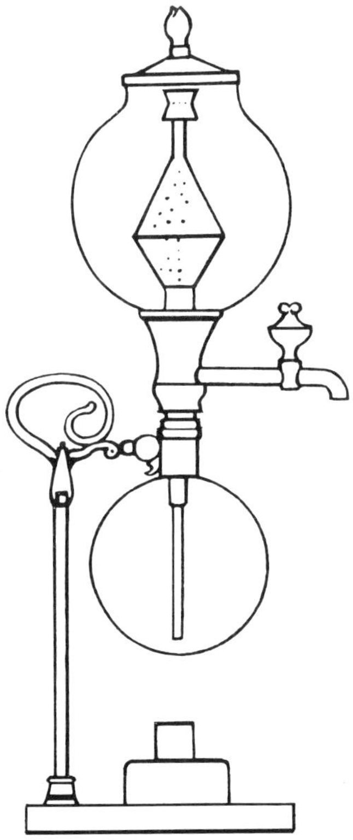

level in the tube, which she called a 'manomètre'. She also changed the shape of the filter to give it a bigger area of surface and more holes.

10

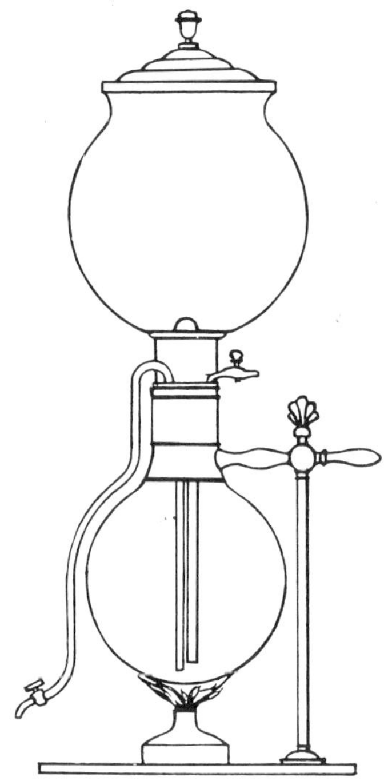

11

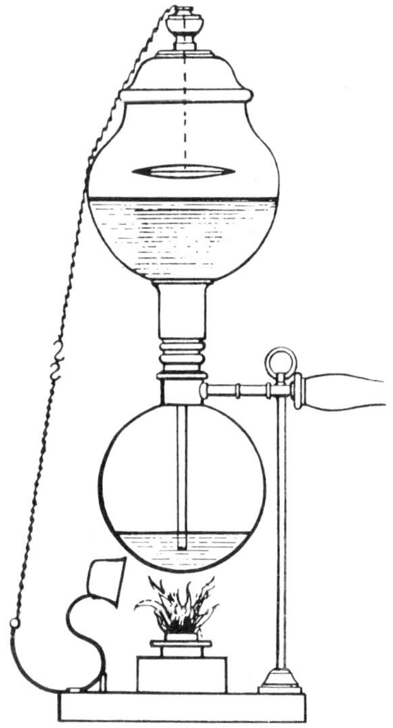

12

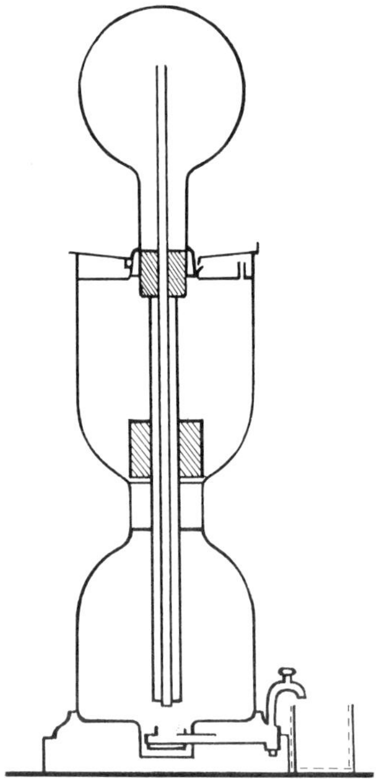

Before the ink was dry on this supplementary application she had thought of another improvement, marked by an asterisk and written in all the way down the margin. "La Dame Massot femme Vassieux has had the happy thought that a dial or clock carrier could be mounted on the collar of the lower flask so that the apparatus can be used both as a clock and coffee maker."

The Vassieux cafetière was certainly put into production since in 1846, just before it expired, it was renewed for fifteen years by her daughter, la Demoiselle Vassieux of 38 rue Vivienne in Paris. The assumption must be that Madame Vassieux had died. Her invention, however, was very much alive, and in 1849 Miss Vassieux improved it. Her address was now the rue du Faubourg-Montmartre where all her competitors were.

In 1842 Rosa Galy-Cazalat also registered in Paris a series of designs which show a completely different arrangement of the flask. Her spirit heater is placed round the neck of the apparatus. The water is heated in the upper flask and then passes through the coffee into the lower one and steam is redirected back into the lamp to extinguish the flame.

The patent was granted to her at the home of her father who was himself an engineer and inventor living in the rue Folie-

10 - The Gosse design of 1842. The second tube with a valve enabled water to be heated in advance. The coffee could then be made quickly when needed.

11 - Fortant's patent has a self-extinguishing mechanism which operates when the liquor rises, pushing up the float. The chain slackens and the lid falls onto the flame. The air in the lower flask cools and the coffee filters back into it.

12 - One of Rosa Galy-Cazalat's series of coffee machine drawings with the spirit heater round the neck of the upper flask. When the water boils, steam extinguishes the flame. Since the cold water starts off in the top, this flask has to be filled first and then the other parts assembled upside down on top of it. The complete apparatus is then reversed and the spirit poured in and lit. Steam forces the water into the top of the central tube and downwards through the box-shaped filter into the lower flask.

13

14

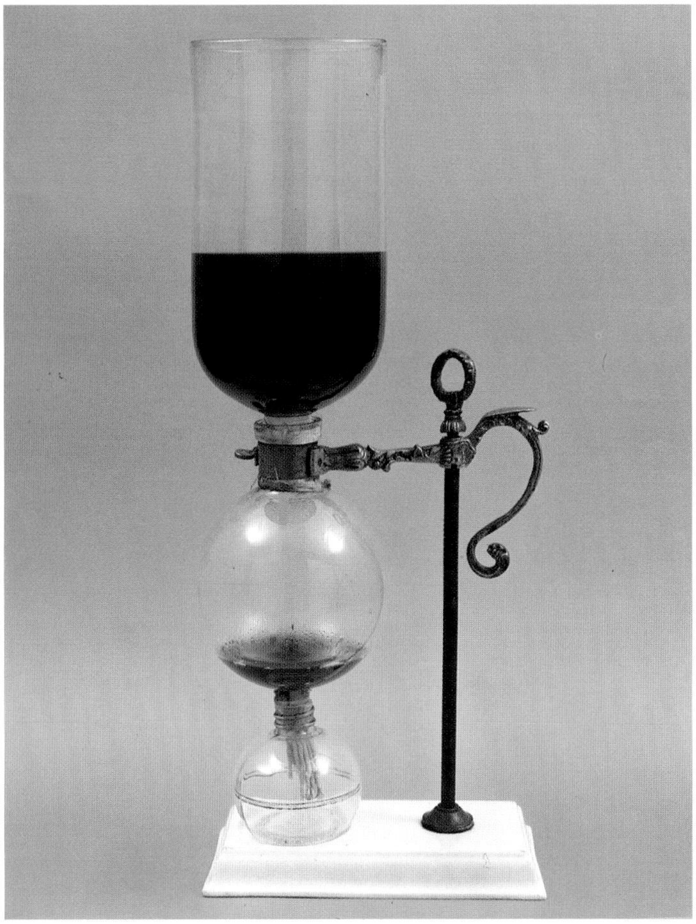

13 - Raparlier type of two-tier machine but with glass upper flask and copper lower boiler with stand and spirit lamp. Bramah Collection.

14 - French double glass vacuum coffee-maker from the 19th century.

Méricourt. He and Professor Galy-Cazalat, a professor of physics at the College of Versailles, produced between them a long series of inventions extending over nearly forty years and covering every aspect of steam, hydraulics and mechanics, gas and electricity. They began in the 1820s at Perpignan with an idea for propelling ships by detonation and ended in 1866 in Paris with a road vehicle powered by a gazogene.

Like Madame Vassieux', Miss Galy-Cazalat's was an invention which was intended to be manufactured commercially, and she added more improvements a year later, still from her father's address, but under her married name of Martres. The drawings are highly professional, noticeably lacking in the decorative little embellishments of the amateur inventor, and the mechanisms are so complicated that Monsieur Galy-Cazalat must have had a hand in them. In fact when the patent was renewed for the last time in 1847 it was in his name.

The success of these Frenchwomen was particularly remarkable because it was achieved in the face of intense competition. Coffee making was no longer dominated by metalsmiths. Everything could

15

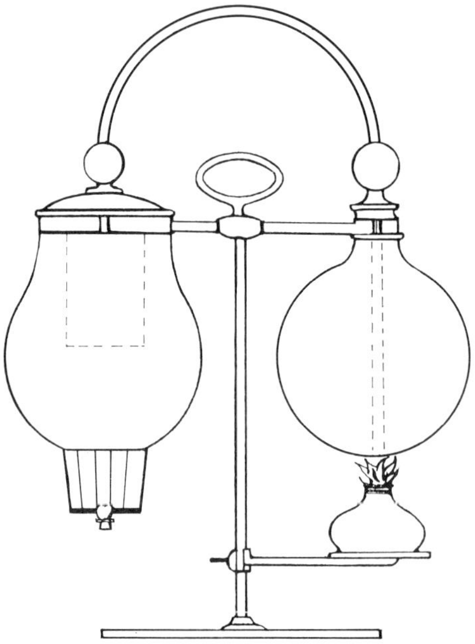

16

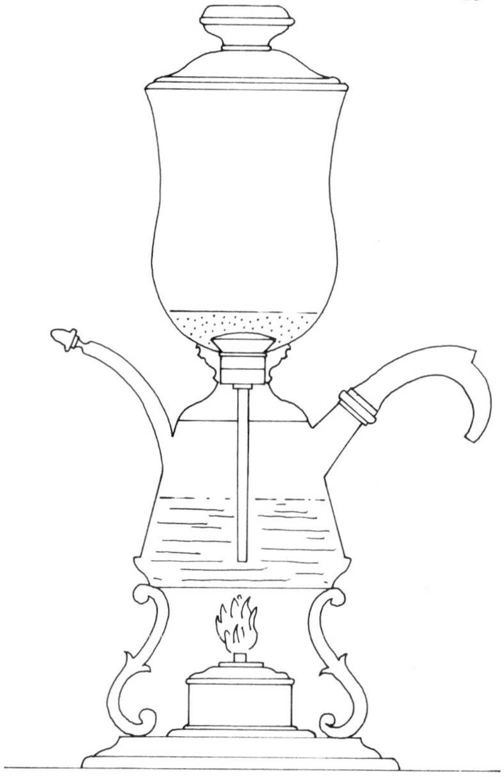

17

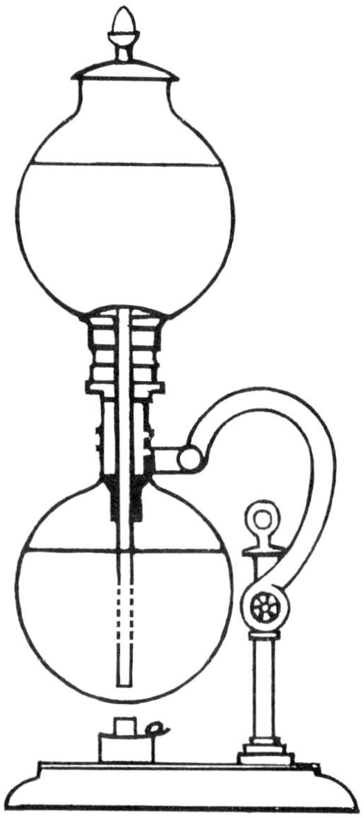

be assembled from components. Cafetières had left the kitchen and were prominently displayed on dining room table or sideboard where their merits and disadvantages were very clearly seen.

Instead of a new patent being registered every few years, a dozen were appearing every year and there were many more which were not original enough to be patented. From the constant references to improved safety, most must have ended up as heaps of shattered glass. All-glass machines reached the limit of their practical variations within about three years and seem suddenly to have lost their dominance to be resurrected fifty years later in America with the advantage of toughened glass and enjoy a new vogue. Because of this comparatively recent revival the machines of the 1840s look startlingly modern, but they were less innovative at that time than they would be to us because they were similar to the oil lamps and gas lamps which also often had two tiers and were completely familiar to the public.

Another factor is very important. These French machines have a superficial similarity because they were glass, but there were significant differences in the way that they worked. Some forced the water through the coffee, others made the water flow over it. Spirit heaters became more and more sophisticated with more than one kind of self - extinguishing device, and there were also different types of non-returning valves to direct the water from one flask to another. Metal coffee makers had used the same complicated mechanisms but they were concealed within the metal casing. Virtually every contribution that had been made to the improved brewing of coffee up to 1840 was translated into a glass machine, and everything was exposed to view. They appealed as an entertainment and on the practical side they were much easier to clean. Also their component parts were replaceable.

18

Their weakness was that they were potentially very dangerous. Breakages were frequent, and either from careless use or a fault in the glass, they were liable to explode. Having passed into the repertoire of coffee makers, they did not disappear entirely, but they were modified. As the nineteenth century progressed the bottom flask was made in metal and the stand at the side disappeared. The designs began to look stodgy and the two-tier coffee machine became just one of many alternatives. The fashionable world meanwhile moved on to something new.

In England, the sturdy and practical Platow machine was the furthest that the British middle classes had been prepared to go. One glass flask was enough. There, other methods of preparing coffee were being tried out.

15 - The lateral arrangement of flasks by Bastien in 1842. The ground coffee is held in a perforated canister attached by a bayonet clip under the lid of the receiving flask.

16 - The Raparlier Excellente was popular in 1856 but compared with its predecessors it was heavy and over-ornate.

17 - The Malpeyre patent of 1841. Part of the stand is detachable to provide a handle. The disadvantage of this machine is that the top had to be removed so that the coffee could be poured.

18 - Glass vacuum coffee-makers with the coffee in different stages of the brewing process.

PUSH AND PULL COFFEE MAKERS

To get boiling water quickly through the coffee, inventors had explored pretty thoroughly the possibilities of forcing it through by steam pressure or drawing it through using the force of a partial vacuum. The disadvantage of both was that the action was sudden and uncontrolled. To get a good extraction in a reasonable time and still have some control over the process a new device appeared, the pneumatic pump.

One of Dr. Romershausen's extraction presses of 1820 used a hand pump as an alternative to steam to send water through vegetable matter, including coffee. Manual force can work two ways, it can push or it can pull. Pushing uses a plunger, pulling requires something very like a syringe. In England the pulling method or exhaustion pump came first.

Brain's vacuum or pneumatic filter of 1835 was in two parts with a mesh in between which was covered with a closely woven cloth or chamois leather like a membrane, making a tight joint. Coffee and then boiling water were put into the top and then the piston of the exhaustion pump was pulled out to draw the liquor through. This was a good and efficient method which was under the operator's control.

A more delicate version was Whitehead's pneumatic coffee pot with the pump in the lid. This had a French patent in 1840, and of course could also be used for making tea. The same exhausting pump appears on Tiesset's patent of 1842. Tiesset lived at Boulogne and so was rather behind the Paris fashion which was for glass cafetières. He was one of many inventors who spent years working on their ideas and enjoyed a modest success but failed to leave a lasting impression.

The counterpart of the exhaustion pump is the piston, and Robert Beart's was the first of these in 1838. Beart was a miller living in the heart of rural England and his machine was more remarkable for strength than elegance. But like the pump, it was very efficient. The outer cylinder was of strong tin or brass and with a piston pierced with holes which was the diameter of the inside of the cylinder. A piece of chamois leather was fitted over the under side to provide resistance while at the same time allowing water to pass through slowly.

To operate the Beart machine, the piston started at the bottom of the pot. Coffee was

1

2

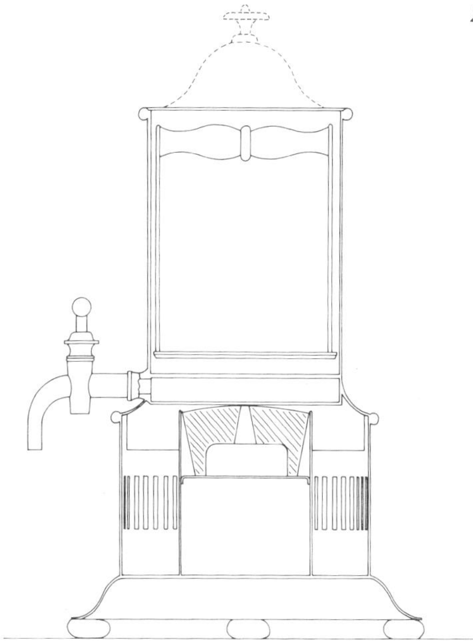

3

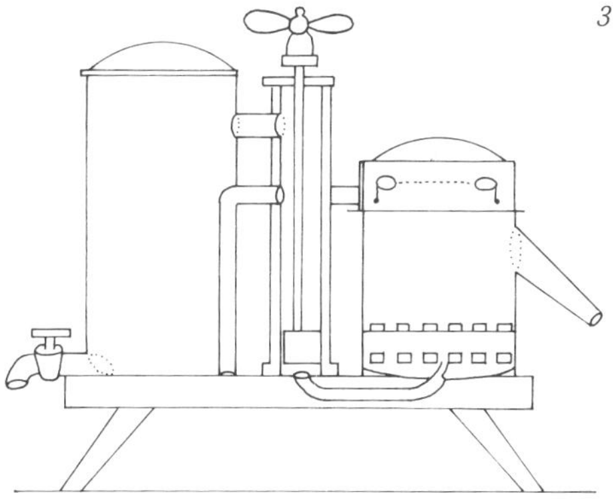

4

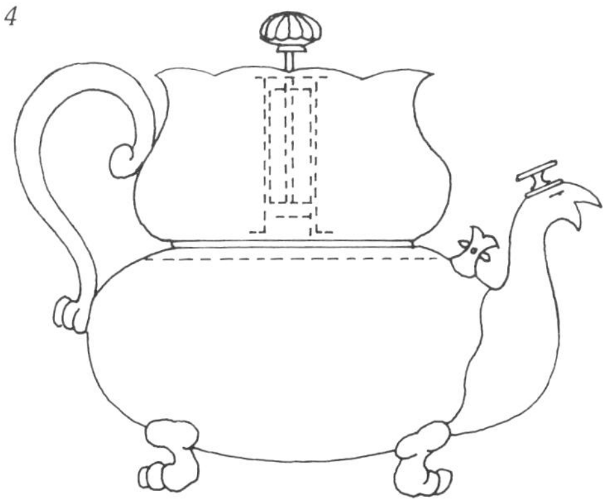

5

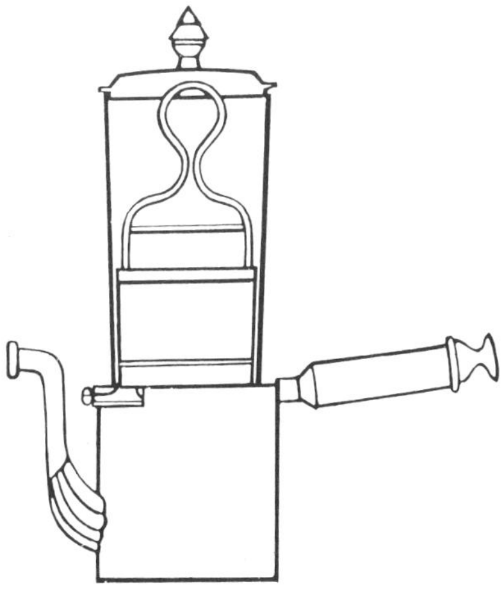

1 - The piston coffee-maker invented by Beart in 1838. He designed a large version which had a winch to raise the piston and a dining room model which worked by hand. Bramah Collection.

2 - Beart's patent design.

3 - One of Romershausen's extraction machines of 1818 with a piston for making coffee in both an urn and a coffee dispenser.

4 - A pretty pot invented by John Whitehead of London in 1840, but patented in Paris through Monsieur Bloque of the Place Dauphine. It has a delicate little syringe which draws the boiling water through the coffee. It was called a cafetière but, probably because White was English, looks like a teapot.

5 - Tiesset's French patent of 1842 with exhaustion pump.

6

7

6/7 - The Ward Andrews piston coffee pot patented in 1841. The flap behind the handle is the entry point for the boiling water which is held in a separate compartment from the body of the pot. A piston pushes it through the coffee grounds.
Bramah Collection. The patent drawing shows the internal arrangement of the pot.

8/9 - Brain's machine of 1835 had a suction pump which drew the water through the coffee when the handle was pulled out. The coffee grounds rested on a mesh inside the upper vase. Bramah Collection.

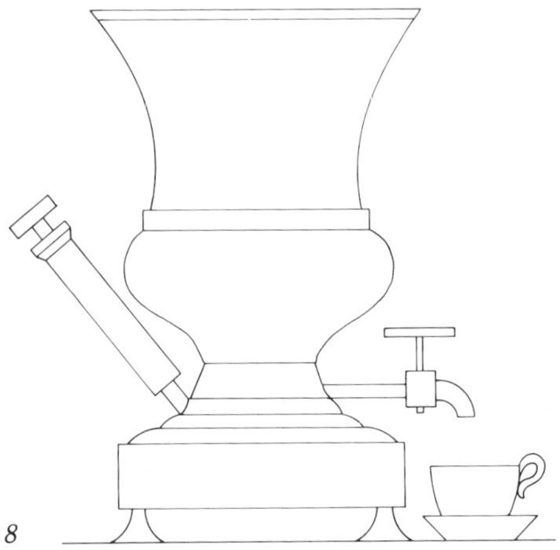

8

9

put in and then boiling water. The piston was raised by means of a handle and the vacuum, which developed between the bottom of the pot and the rising piston, pulled the liquor through.

There were several versions of Beart's machine ranging from a large model which used a winch to raise the piston down to a little brass or copper one intended for the dining room. The pressure of the water gave a very good extraction from the coffee, but the disadvantage of the design was that the piston was left in the raised position which was not very attractive. One solution was a smaller piston. The 1841 machine of William Ward Andrews achieved this. Andrews was an ironmonger of Wolverhampton. His piston was in a separate column next to the handle of the pot. Boiling water was poured into the column with the piston completely raised and the piston pushed it down and through the coffee into the body of the pot.

Manual piston machines had many advantages. They were safe, simple to operate and unlikely to alarm the servants, but they never enjoyed lasting popularity. There was no way of using them gracefully. Anybody either pushing or pulling a piston was immediately revealed as all elbows.

10

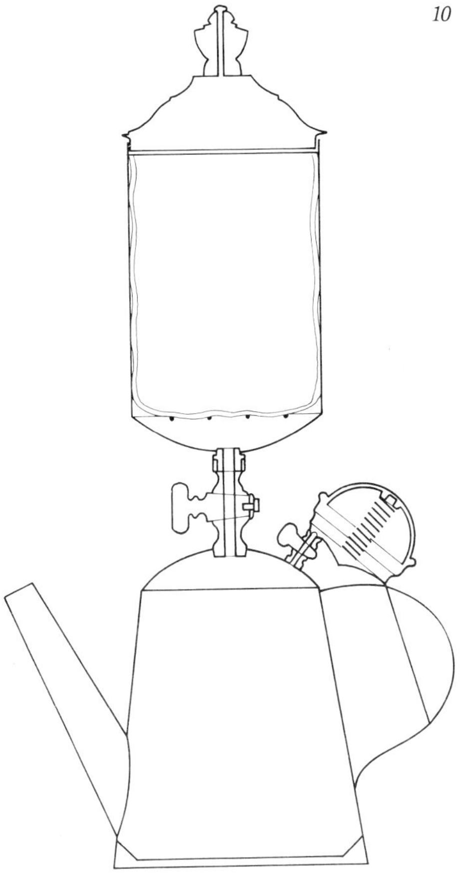

10 - Lavater's patent of 1874 which used a rubber diaphragm which was pressed several times to speed up the filtering action of the liquor. The top section contained a bag which held the coffee grounds while they infused. The join between the top and bottom section was so narrow that the machine was easily broken as were also the coffee makers which used exhaustion pumps.

The Lavater patent of 1873 was an attempt to combine the biggin with a coffee pot. It was activated by means of a rubber diaphragm and spring which was pressed several times to induce the liquor to pass through.

It was a drip pot in which the filtering process was speeded up by adding a little vacuum power as an encouragement. Like the others, it was complicated to manufacture, offered few opportunities to craftsmen and did not pretend to be automatic.

But it really stood no chance because it was in competition with a machine which was the classic British coffee maker throughout nearly the whole of the reign of Queen Victoria, the Napierian.

THE NAPIERIAN

The most enduring and typical of all nineteenth-century English coffee-makers was designed during the 1840s by a marine engineer, but it was never patented since it was really made up of standard laboratory equipment and did not have the artful little valves and stoppers which are necessary to claim uniqueness.

The inventor was a member of the Napier family who founded the great Scottish shipbuilding industry on the River Clyde. Robert Napier was born in Dumbarton in 1791 and constructed his first marine engine in 1823 in Glasgow. His early work was on cross-Channel steamers and this attracted the attention of Samuel Cunard who was planning a transatlantic line. Their collaboration formed the basis of the shipbuilding firm of Robert Napier and Sons at Govan. One of these sons was James Napier who not only continued the traditional company business of marine engineering but also developed a sideline of his own in kitchen equipment, and in particular a coffee maker. It was only a small achievement in a distinguished career, but because it was simple, durable and capable of being made a thing of beauty by generations of silversmiths, it lasted right through the reign of Queen Victoria and beyond.

1

1 - James Napier of the shipbuilding company of Robert Napier and Sons, engineer and inventor of the Napierian coffee machine in the early 1840s.

2 - The basic Napierian put together from simple components. Boiling water was added to grounds in the beaker and the liquor was made to syphon back into the flask.

3 - Silver-plated version dismantled ready to pour the coffee. Marked T Smith & Son, Glasgow. Height 34cms. Bramah Collection.

The Napierian, as it came to be called, was not complicated in its original form although it did have a rather medical look about it which did not however prove any handicap to its success. The increasingly prosperous British middle classes very much preferred it to the frivolities which were emerging at that time from the France of Louis Philippe.

2

3

4 - *Late Victorian silver-plated Napier machine with serving tap engraved with the "willow pattern". Made by William Padley & Son of Sheffield. Height 37cms. Bramah Collection.*

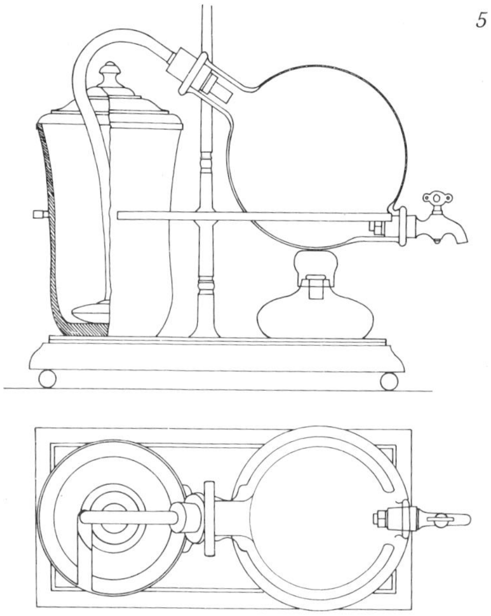

5 - *Patent drawing of Robertson's 'improvement' of the Napier machine in 1890 in which he has added a serving tap to the glass flask.*

It was very simple to operate. Boiling water was poured over coffee grounds in a jar and a little boiling water was put into a globe. The two vessels were connected by a metal tube which passed through a stopper in the neck of the globe to make an air-tight joint. At the jar end of the tube was a strainer. The whole apparatus was mounted on a stand with a spirit heater under the globe to boil the small volume of water and create steam which passed through the tube and agitated the coffee and kept up the temperature. When the spirit heater was taken away, the air in the globe condensed, forming a partial vacuum, and the coffee liquor was drawn back leaving the grounds behind. The globe was released from its stopper and tube and then became the coffee pot. The jar could be glass, ceramic or metal but the globe was most commonly glass. It was not a fully automatic machine since the water had to be boiled separately, but the brewing action was very fast.

Napier was too engaged in the family shipbuilding company to manufacture his machine himself, but he never lost interest in it. It was gradually refined to lose its clinical appearance, though not without some resistance from Napier. In 1870, Thomas Smith & Son were making the machine under his personal direction. Since they were silversmiths, they felt that they had some important contributions to make, which led to a row with old Mr. Napier who told old Mr. Smith, "You may be a guid silversmith, but I am a better engineer."

By 1860 the Napier machine was being exported to India, China and the United States as well as Europe, and won prizes at many trade exhibitions. It was stocked by stores and ironmongers all over Britain and there was a brisk trade in spares. Although the surviving price lists emphasise that the glass flask (replacement price about eight pence) was very safe, it required some care in handling, particularly in frosty weather when boiling water was most liable to shatter the glass. With a little experience it

7

6/7 - Silversmiths' adaptations of the Napier machine. The globe now has lateral pins which fit into supports.
Left: a small and very beautiful Napierian in silver plate. No mark. Height 34 cms.

Above: a model made by Thomas Smith & Son of Glasgow. Original cork fitting suggest an early model. Later ones more usually had a plated screw connecting the tube to the golbe. Bramah Collection.

8 - Very fine Padley silver-plated Napier machine with match-box and spirit bottle to hold a week's supply of spirit for the heater. Height 37cms. City of Sheffield Museum.

9 - Another Padley machine of the same period from the Bramah Collection.

10 - Napierian with tall vertical supports and lamp snuffer. Marked Roberts and Belk, Sheffield. Height 38cms. Bramah Collection.

11 - Napierian with flask supported on four legs with lion claw feet. Marked Roberts and Belk. c. 1890. Height 37 cms. Bramah Collection.

8

was possible to avoid using a spirit lamp altogether by pouring boiling water into the flask to heat it, emptying it out and then quickly pressing the stopper and end of the tube into the neck. This was sufficient to begin the syphoning action which drew back the liquor.

The cheapest 2-pint size Napier machine with glass jar and flask was 65p, and the most expensive 4-pint size with a gilt-edged china jar, German silver tube and cut glass spirit lamp was just over £3. There was a half-gallon size for clubs and cafés and a catering model which had two flasks flanking a single jar which produced continuous supplies of coffee. For the carriage trade there was plated silver. These show most clearly how the design developed over the years into the large late-Victorian Napierian with a serving tap.

Athough Napier did not patent his machine, other people registered their improvements. Robertson's of 1890 merely added a tap to the flask.

The Napierian was popular for more than sixty years and many silver-plated ones still exist, but knowledge of how they worked disappeared astonishingly quickly. An antique dealer who has one among his stock is quite likely to have no idea even that the machine makes coffee, and even back in the 1940s when there were many people still alive who would have used them, this had begun to happen. In 1943 the 'Ironmonger' published a letter headed "What is this?" describing a strange silver-plated mechanism engraved with the willow pattern. Among the replies was one from a Mr. Arthur Padley, aged 63, and helping in the war effort by working in a steel mill in Sheffield. As a boy, he had spent a few years in his father's firm of William Padley and Son who had been silversmiths in Sheffield for generations until they went out of business when the silver trade was badly hit at the beginning of the twentieth century by the South African war. He had recognised the willow pattern as one of the favourite family engraving designs. It is a rather poignant example of the way in which a tradition of craftsmanship can run into financial disaster. Many surviving silver-plated Napier machines carry Padley marks and can be dated within a few years by the changes in the initials as the company amalgamated and developed in the nineteenth century.

A Napierian looks superb on a sideboard and they are quite unjustly neglected. They are nearly always in complete working order, needing only to be thoroughly cleaned, and they can be relied on to make the excellent coffee they always did.

MATCHES

10

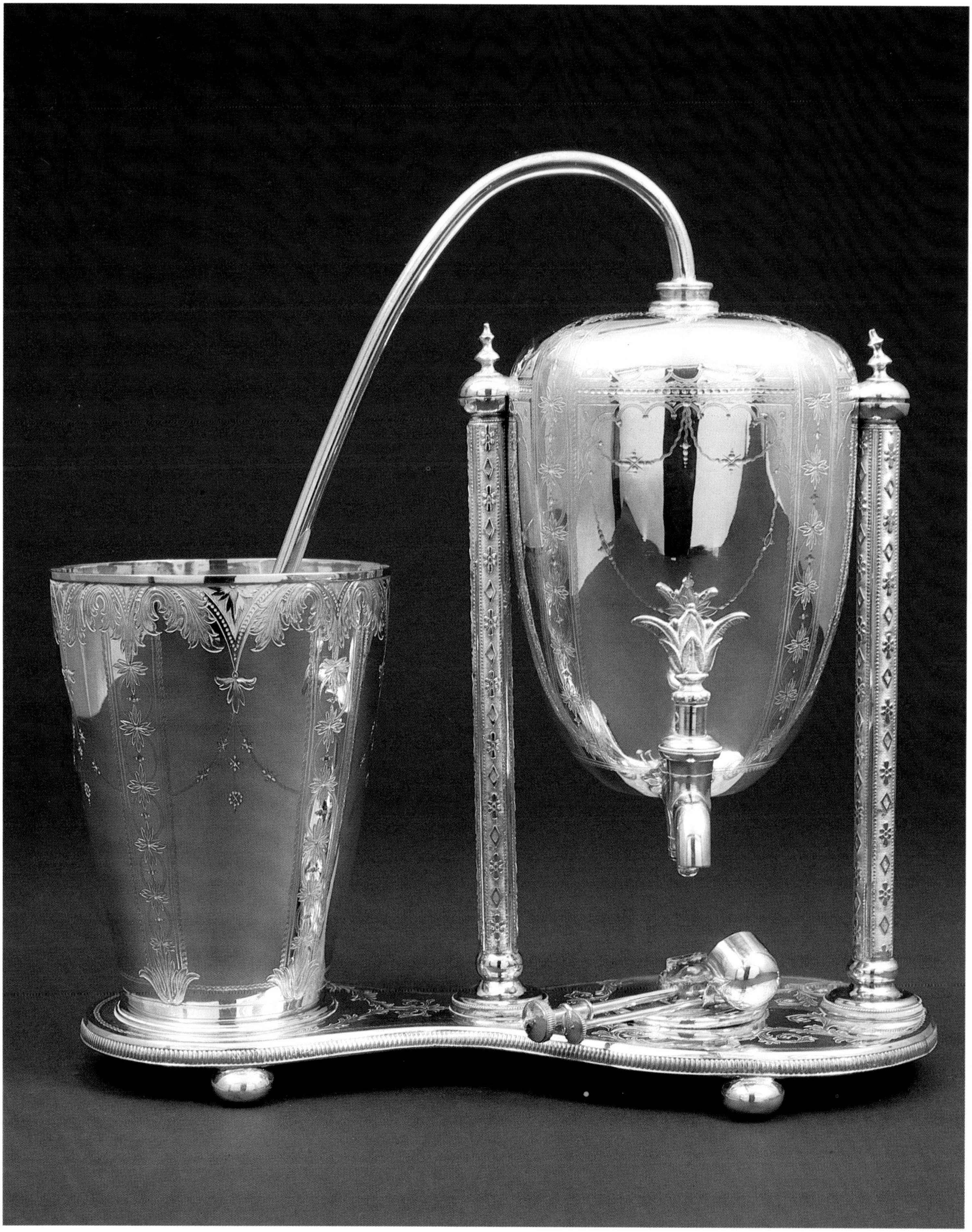

11

BALANCING SYPHONS

The French double glass machine was a phenomenon which had not completely succeeded, but on the other hand had by no means failed. Price lists for the flasks for Napier machines make it clear that thin-blown glass of the mid-nineteenth century was capable of withstanding quite easily any amount of boiling water, but they did require care. Inventors had great confidence in them since they took out patents for fifteen years, but they were really ahead of glass technology. They did not have the heat-proof glass that coffee machine manufacturers have available to them today. Also, the enormous interest in coffee making in the early 1840s had its own inevitable consequence: fashionable Paris moved on to something new.

The Bastien patent of 1842, one example of which still exists in Paris, is the link between the two-tier machine and the next fashion, which was the balancing syphon. Bastien's is a double glass machine with the two flasks arranged side-by-side instead of one above the other. The boiling water is forced through a filter box containing the coffee into the second flask fitted with a tap. The necks of both flasks are held by a single cross-piece, and this is not only more stable, but puts both the heater and the serving tap at the same convenient level. The only thing it lacks is a method of

1

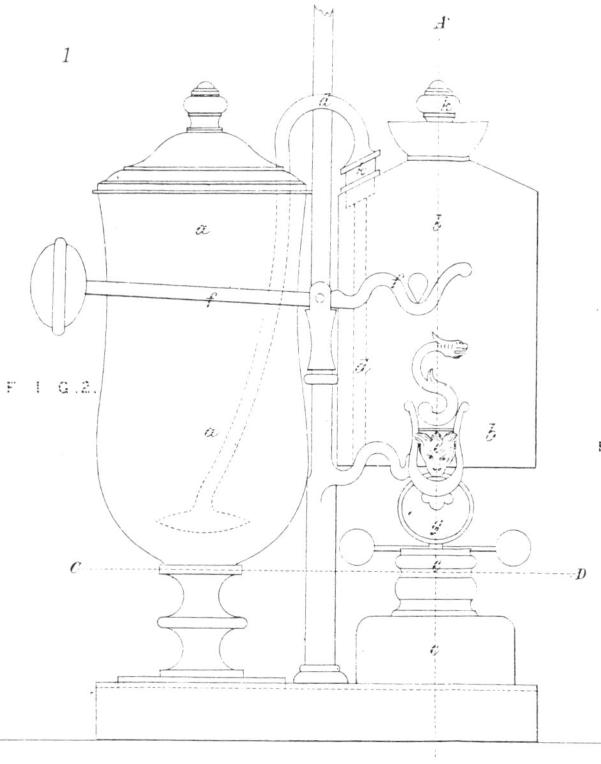

2

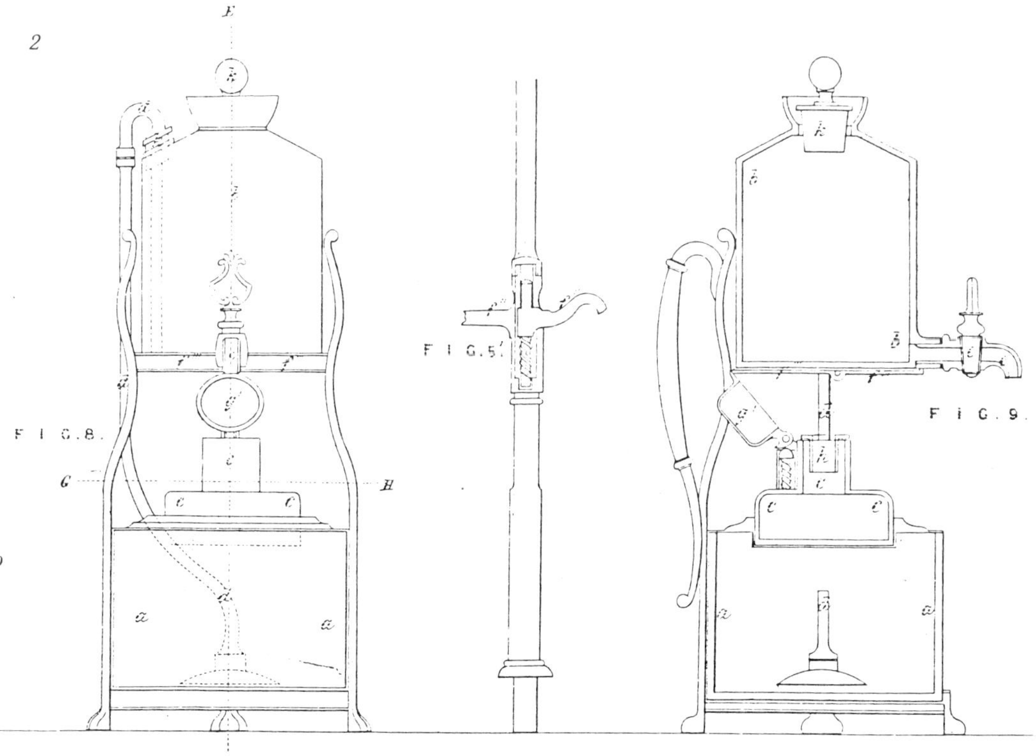

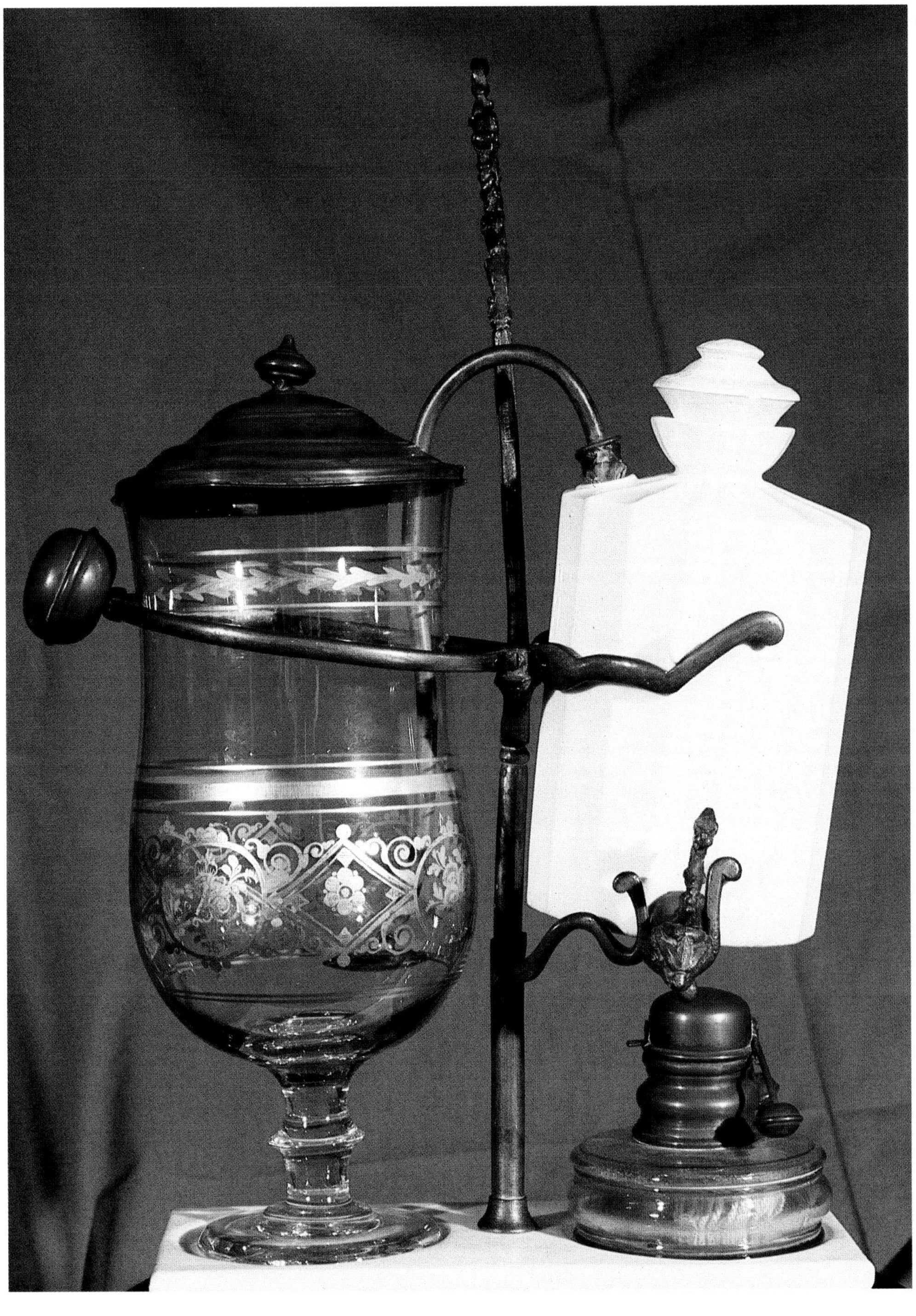
3

1 - Balancing syphon intended for the English market and patented in London by Preterre of Le Havre in 1849. He copied Godet's simple counterpoise. Reiss of Vienna brought out a similar version at about the same time.

2 - Preterre's alternative balancing syphon in which the two flasks are positioned one above the other with the heater in between.
The lid is held open by the upper flask when it is full of water. The cold water is heated and forced by steam pressure through the tube into the bottom to mix with the coffee. The top flask then rises on a spring in the stand which holds it, the air inside cools and the coffee is drawn back.

3 - Balancing syphon with weighted counterpoise. This one has a beautifully gilded flask. Some had porcelain jars decorated with flowers and birds on a blue ground in the manner of Sèvres and Limoges.
Lavazza Collection, Turin.

automatically extinguishing the heat, and this improvement followed almost immediately.

Balancing syphons outlasted Louis Philippe and went right through into the Second Empire. Like the double-glass cafetière, they all have a superficial resemblance but there were many variations. With persistence, it is still possible to collect most of them, but anyone wishing to do so should hurry while they are still available. The one in the Science Museum in London was found sitting, unrecognised, on the mantelpiece of a curator's office, but that was a few years ago and their days of obscurity are over.

Balancing syphons combined maximum efficiency with the maximum visual appeal. They provided inventors with years of harmless fun and became popular all over Europe. They are sometimes described as 'Viennese syphon machines'. As in the case of the glass double-flask machines, it is difficult to discover the exact moment when they first appeared since documentary evidence only begins when they are improved, but in France they were often known as a "gabet" and Louis Gabet, who had a workship in the Marais district of Paris, took out a patent in 1844. He did not claim ownership of the entire construction of the balancing syphon but he did give a complete description of it and he added a statement at the end of his specification that he would defend his counterpoise device by legal action if necessary. The Gabet model with the counterpoise was one of the more successful forms of balancing syphon, and the way it worked is as follows.

4

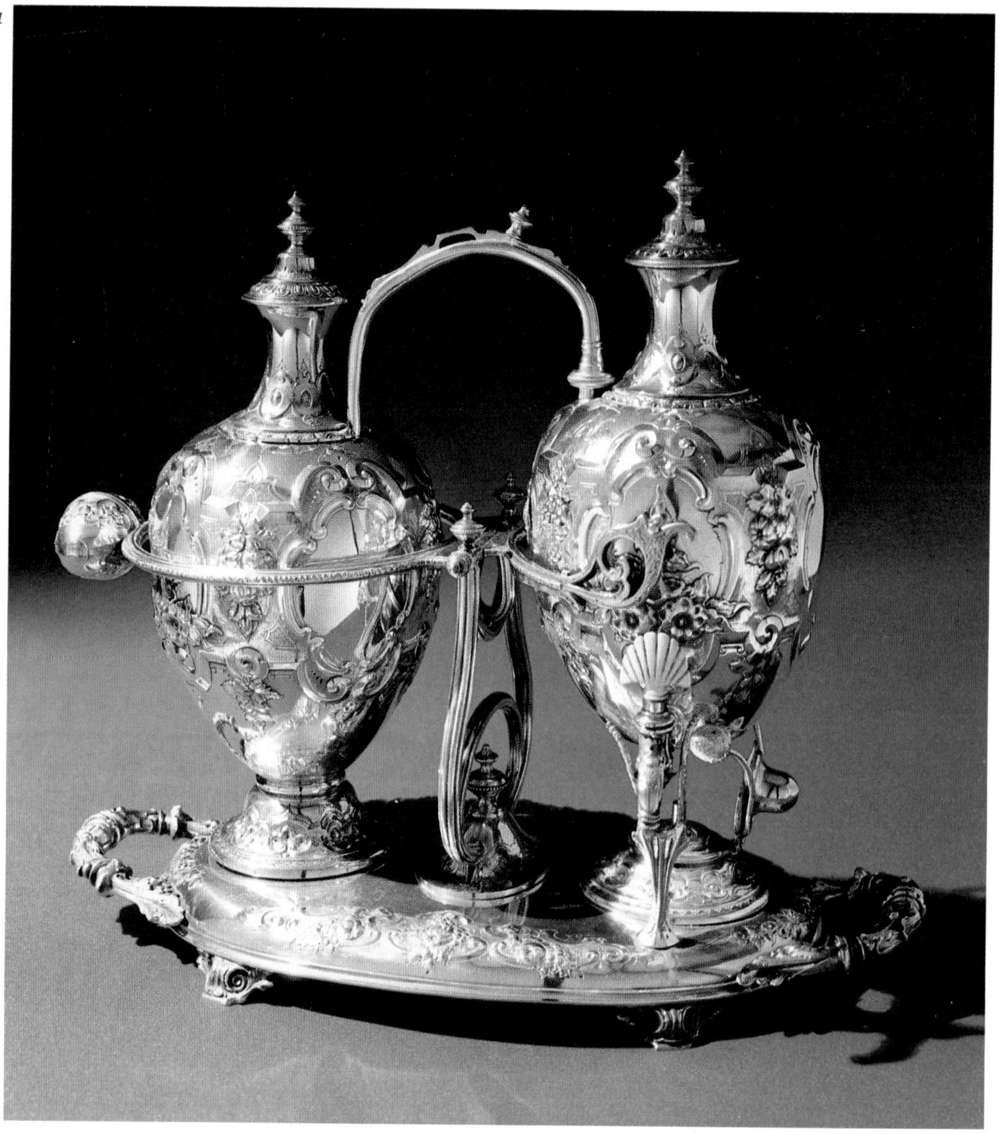

The weight of the cold water in the right hand container, which was commonly ceramic, held open the lid of the spirit lamp. When the water passed over into the glass flask the empty jar rose, assisted by the counterpoise action of the weight attached to the ring around the flask. The lid was released and flipped shut to extinguish the flame. The air in the jar then cooled and the partial vacuum drew back the coffee, causing the jar to descend again.

The superior merits of the balancing syphon hardly need stating. It was extremely safe, it was completely automatic and it offered great opportunities to manufacturers of metal stands, painted china and gilded glass. There were soon dozens of people - doctors, mathematicians, pharmacists and café proprietors as well as metalsmiths and glass makers - who crowded in with their improvements to the balancing mechanism and arrangements of the syphon tube. Turmel's quite late patent of 1853 shows that it was possible to make a perfectly simple design very complicated.

The balancing syphon even came to England where Apoleoni Pierre Preterre of le Havre sent Greeting to her most Excellent Majesty Queen Victoria in a patent of 1849. England, with its increasingly prosperous middle classes, must have looked very attractive to Preterre where the rest of Europe was collapsing into revolution behind him. His specification is an omnibus package which includes a roasting apparatus and coffee mill as well as a balancing syphon with a counterpoise similar to Gabet's. A very interesting feature is the alternative two-tier version with the spirit lamp between them. It would be very interesting to know if an example of this still exists.

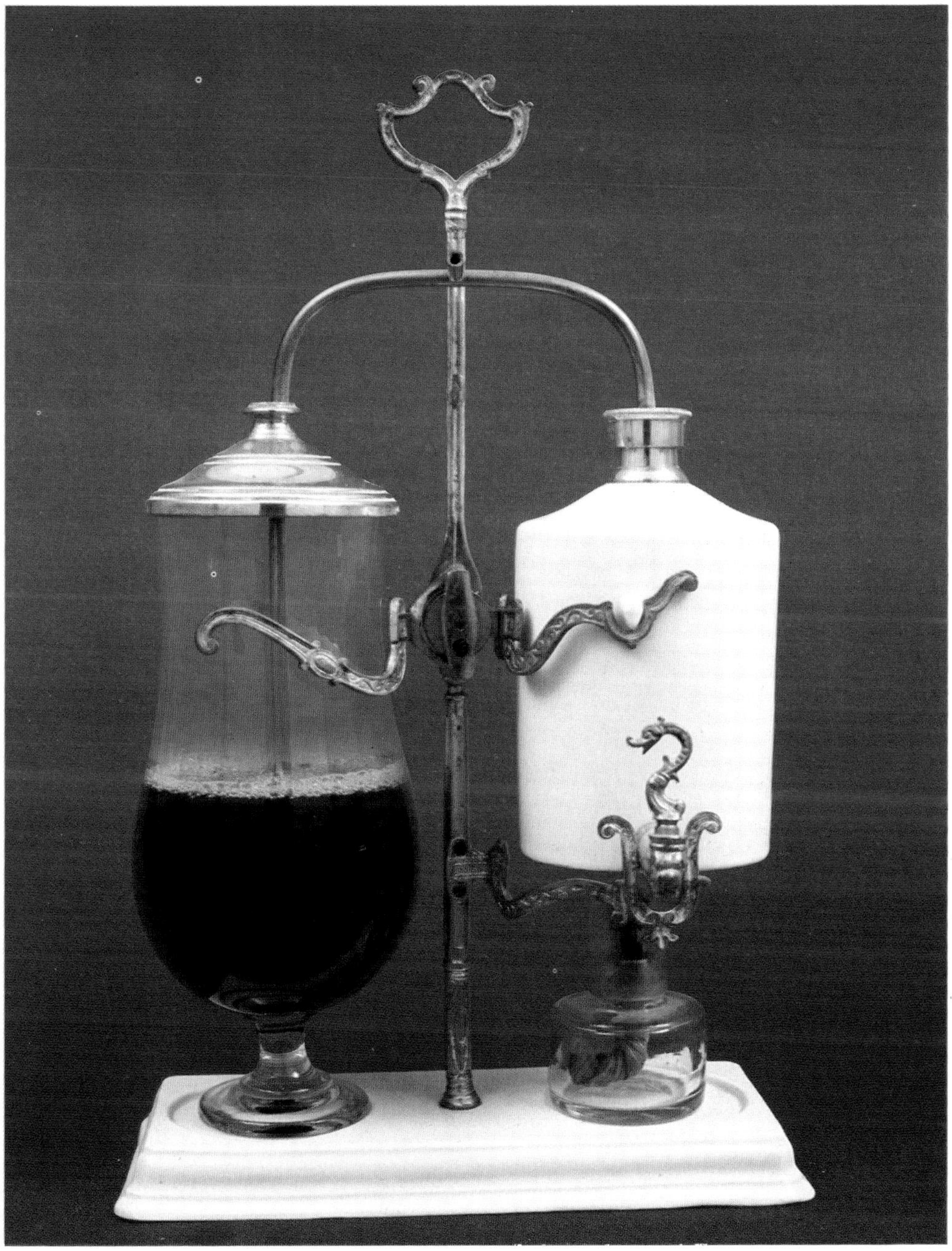

5

6

7

4 - Ornate silver-plated English balancing syphon from the late nineteenth century. It works on the Gabet principle with a heavy weight acting as a counterpoise. Maker unknown. Bramah Collection.

5 - Balancing syphon with coil spring mechanism to help raise the empty porcelain jar and release the lid of the heater. In this model, the tube goes from the middle of the top of the jar to the middle of the top of the flask. There were about a dozen different possible arrangements of the component parts and examples exist of most of them. Bramah Collection.

6 - Syphon with gilded support frame and porcelain jar painted with sprigs of flowers. The central column contains a spring which extends from the arms supporting the jar down to the base. Bramah Collection.

7 - Patent drawing of the Turmel balancing syphon of 1853. By this time French adaptations had become very complicated. The serving flask rests on a shelf which is raised with the assistance of a hydraulic lift. The connection between the tube and the upper part of the flask has also been equipped with a system of valves and vents. Over a number of years, Turmel invented a series of a dozen coffee machines using very sophisticated mechanisms.

COFFEE LOCOMOTIVES

Today, steam locomotives are objects of nostalgia. In Europe in the 1830s they were inspiration. Long before the main transcontinental lines were constructed to join up the major cities, railway trains were all the rage. Pictures of them were published in hundreds of thousands and transfer printed onto masses of plates and mugs as souvenirs. In Paris and Vienna coffee-machines designed as locomotives began to appear.

The first railway line in France was opened in 1837 to run from Paris to St. Germain. In February 1839 Adolphe Darru wrote to the Minister of Commerce applying for a patent for a coffee-maker in the form of a locomotive. He made it clear that he wanted it in a hurry and it was granted the next month. Darru was a silversmith with a showroom and workshop at 134 rue Montmartre and it can be safely assumed that the little train was to be made in silver. Only some of his drawings are still available, but it is quite clear that it works on the same principle as the Parker Steam Fountain or Vienna Incomparable, forcing the boiling water up through a coffee container and into a second compartment. There was even a little glass dome to show when the coffee was being made. The train had a safety valve concealed by the funnel, a whistle and a flag which rose as the level of the coffee rose. It was a thoroughly delightful and efficient little machine and there is every chance that some examples may still exist.

Soon afterwards, in 1840, a similar toy appeared in Vienna where the first line out to the suburbs had been laid in 1838. It was designed by two engineers named Wagenmann and Böttger who were responsible, separately and together, for a number of very varied patents and this particular one also includes a drip pot with internal chimney and milk heater which is almost identical to the Koch coffee maker of 1838, and a pressure pot which is just like Lebrun's of the same year. The locomotive, however, is quite different from Darru's and this raises an interesting question: since they did not hesitate to appropriate designs virtually unaltered from other countries, were they unaware of it or did they think their internal arrangement for the brewing mechanism was better? The Wagenmann locomotive had considerable success and became very well-known at the time, probably because they were prepared to sell licences to anyone who wanted to manufacture it. Darru's, of course, was only

1

1 - English silver-plated model locomotive named Victoria. It was based on the "Firefly" class locomotive created for the new Great Western line, and made as a coffee urn originally for the Queen's Hotel at Swindon Station and now in the Swindon Railway Museum. It has the royal coat of arms on the side of the rear section and a crown. Swindon Railway Museum.

2

2 - Viennese locomotive of 1840 by Wagenmann and Böttger. This version has a completely different mechanism. The boiler in the centre also warms the milk in the compartment on the right. The coffee is made in the drip pot on the left. The funnel holds matches and a little bottle of spirit for the heater. It is a good arrangement for a coffee machine, but as a locomotive it is rather odd. It is approximately 20cms long and 28cms in height.

made in his own workshop. Wagenmann coffee locomotives were made in silver plate and brass and had a syphon tube which deposited the boiling water into the top of a drip pot in the rear. There was a milk heater, and the lid of the funnel had holes in it for storing matches. The specification points out that the mechanism could be adapted to the form of a steamship, but none of these have been discovered and again it would be interesting to know if any were ever made.

England, which by this time had an extensive railway network in construction all over the country, followed with a particularly magnificent train, but this, again, was entirely different. It was made in silver plate to commemorate the opening of the Great Western line from London to Bristol and is based on a Gooch broad-gauge locomotive of the 'Firefly' class. It was unlike the others because only one of them was made and it was a large catering model. It was really an urn and did not have any mechanism to move the water from one place to another. Brunel, the great engineer responsible for the Great Western line, thought that the coffee in the refreshment room at Swindon Station was dreadful, but it is not known whether it came from this locomotive.

3

4

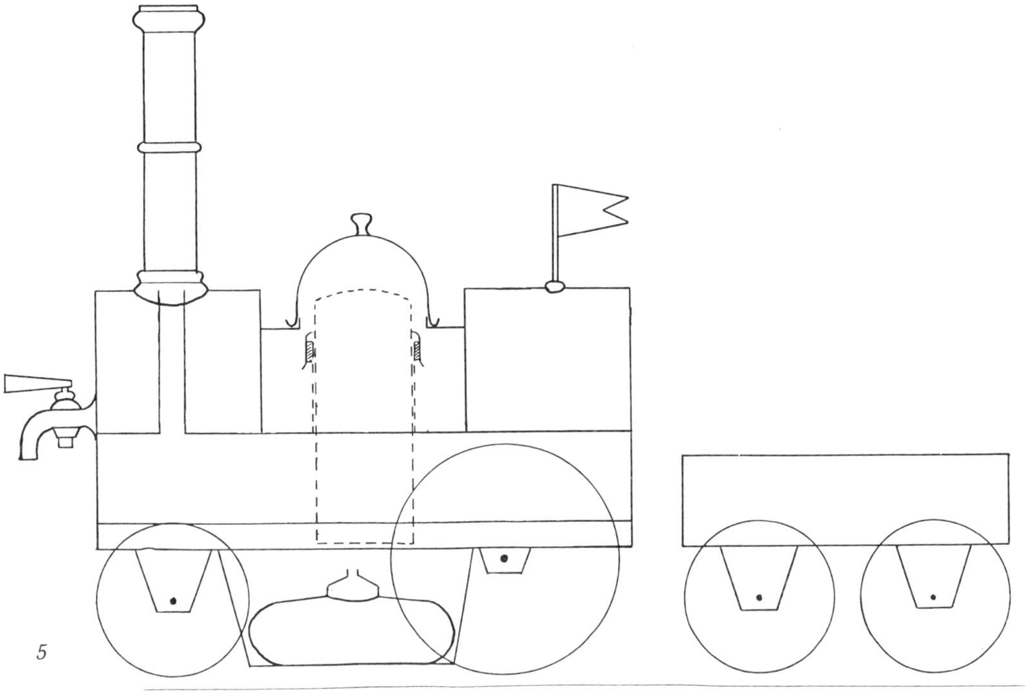

5

3/4 - Two versions of the Vienna locomotive.
Above: in German silver with ornate chassis and its own length of track. Courtesy Folger Coffee Company, U.S.A.
Below: In brass on a wooden chassis. Courtesy of Braunschweig & Co., Basle.

5 - A mechanical toy for the rich. Design drawing of the first "cafetière-locomotive" patented by Adolphe Darru in 1839 to celebrate the opering of the first railway service from Paris to the suburbs. Darru was a silversmith with a showroom in the rue Montmartre and this little train would have been silver plated. It had a little track and also a tender to hold spoons and sugar lumps.

Twenty years passed before the next coffee locomotive appeared, and this was the most interesting of them all. Jean Baptiste Toselli was an architect living in Paris and he was certainly Italian since he signed himself with a 'G' for Giovanni. His first design dated from 1862 and shows a syphon tube taking the water from the rear container to the front and into the funnel. The locomotive sat in its little frame over a spirit heater and when the coffee was made, the heater had to be taken away so that the coffee would syphon back. A tube under the body of the train connected with a tap.

The design is very attractive and makes more sense as a train than Wagenmann and Böttger's. The funnel is large, partly to admit the strainer on the end of the syphon tube and also because the coffee machine was intended to be made in ceramics. The syphon tube was glass so that the water could be seen passing through it and then the coffee syphoning back. It was similar to the balancing syphon, and two years later an extension to the patent adds a balancing mechanism for extinguishing the spirit lamp automatically.

By this time Toselli had had time to manufacture some locomotives and consider extending their possibilities. He had begun to think of it as an educational toy and added some embellishments. The glass tube was twisted like a corkscrew to make the moment when the coffee passed through it more amusing. There was a tender to carry sugar, chocolates, cigars and spoons and some models had a little statuette of a driver while others had a china sugar box. There were several alternative arrangements for the mechanism and although some were syphons, others were simple infusion pots.

These ceramic trains are not common. None of them that were known to be in England bore any maker's name and their origin seemed to be completely obscure, even to the major auction houses, until the authors discovered one in the Elton Collection at the Ironbridge Gorge Museum in Shropshire. Incised on the underside of the ceramic body was the mark 'Toselli & Co' and the metal chassis was stamped 'breveté'. A search revealed the original patent in Paris with the complete range of designs.

Apart from the ceramic trains which are all made in heavy earthenware on a brass or silver plated chassis, it is now clear that there were also metal versions of the Toselli design. Superficially there is little resemblance, but a comparison of the mechanism with the patent drawings reveals that they too are Toselli designs, but probably not carried out in Toselli's workshops.

Toselli was not merely an inventor of toys with a difference. He went on to manufacture coffee machines with a more conventional appearance, registering them in England and Italy as well as France, although his address is always given as Paris. None of them was nearly as charming as the locomotives.

Looking at the cafetière locomotive, one cannot help wondering why the space age has failed to inspire anything with such wit and elegance.

6

7

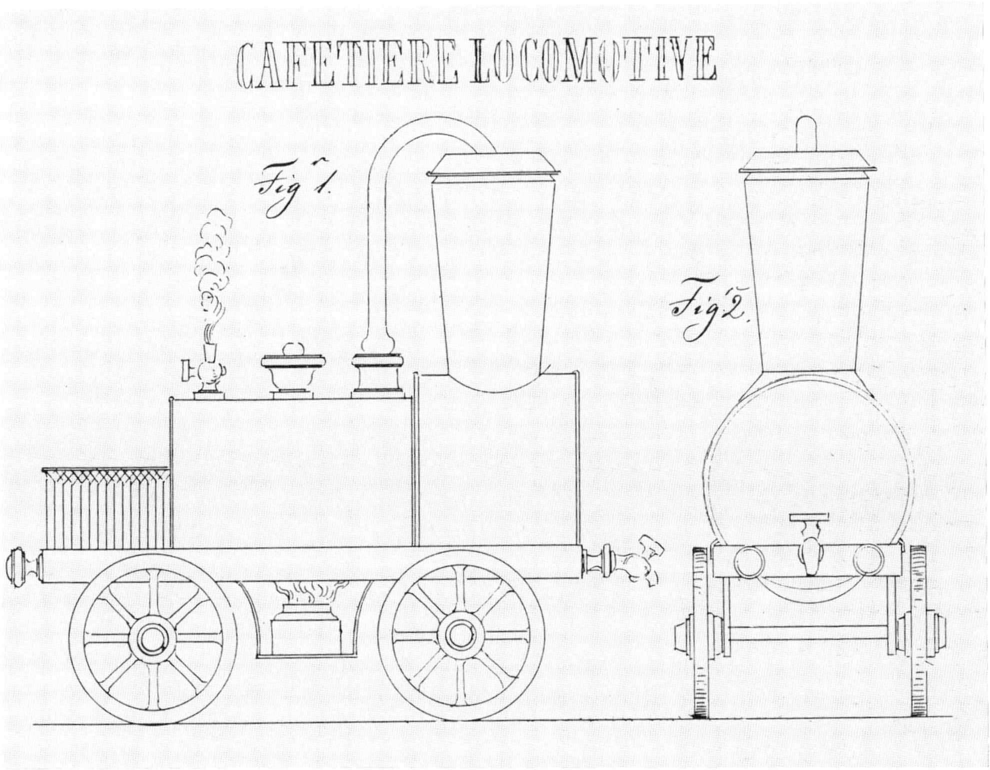

8

6 - The Toselli train in heavy earthenware, pink glaze with hand-painted floral decoration. It rests on its chassis in such a way that it can tip backwards when the rear boiler is full of water to hold open the lid of the spirit lamp, and then tip forward when the weight of the water transfers to the front section, releasing the lid.
Every known example is decorated differently and some have girls' names, initials or family crests surrounded by wreaths of flowers. There is often a matching sugar box instead of a driver. Length 36cms, height 38cms. Bramah Collection.

7 - English silver-plated locomotive made from the Toselli designs. The mechanism is the same as the ceramic version, but the silversmith has been given discretion to adapt the outward appearance. Length, 39 cms. Height 35cms. Bramah Collection.

8 - The first 1862 drawing by Toselli for a model locomotive which makes coffee.
The syphon tube was made of glass to show the coffee passing through. The safety valve was a whistle. In 1864 he patented a series of more complicated designs.

THE HYDROSTATIC PERCOLATOR

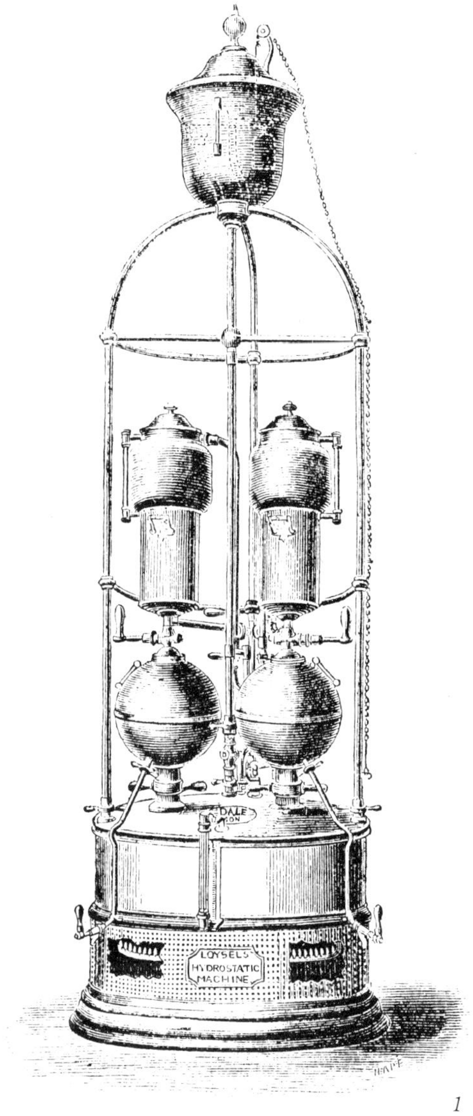

1

1 - The hydraulic coffee-maker extended to its fullest possible extent. This machine was capable of serving thousands of cups of coffee, but was never much more than a curiosity as it took a great deal of skill to operate it.

2 - Silver-plated Loysel machine showing engraved detail. Similar models to this were made from 1856 to the end of the nineteenth century and usually have Loysel's name inside with the stamp of the manufacturer. Bramah Collection.

By the end of the 1840s it must have seemed that every possible method of brewing coffee had been explored. All over Europe a bewildering selection of coffee makers in metal, glass and ceramics was on sale and every year brought more. Most were novelties, difficult to operate and soon abandoned. From the drawings, the first ones invented by Eduard Loysel de la Lantais are not particularly different from a dozen others but he finally achieved great success because he found a principle which was capable of producing coffee on the grandest scale.

The hydraulic paradox is all about the enormous natural pressure of water. If there are two containers side by side, one narrow and the other broad, connected at the base, the water level in both will be the same. If water is poured into the narrower vessel, it will push up the heavier weight of water in the broader one until they are again at the same level. In 1647 Blaise Pascal explained the physical laws which are the basis of the hydraulic press and all other fluid-powered devices. He even drew a diagram of a machine which illustrated the hydraulic paradox, which he called the use of hydrostatic pressure for the magnification of forces, but being a theoretician and not a practical engineer, he took it no further and for a long time neither did anyone else.

Those who knew about it had no use for it, and those who could have used a lifting machine in the mills and docks never got to hear about it. In the English industrial revolution, hydraulic power started to be used for raising heavy weights, but only Loysel saw its application to making coffee since by profession he was a civil engineer.

Eduard Loysel de la Lantais was a Frenchman, born in Vannes in Britanny in 1816, and his father and grandfather were engineers in charge of roads and bridges. From 1838 to 1840 he was Professor of Natural Philosophy and Industrial Mechanics in Marseilles and wrote several books on mechanics, but his main career was as an inventor, selling the rights to his machines to manufacturers in France and England. From 1844 he had a home in England and he became a naturalised British citizen in 1849 but continued to spend a great deal of his time in France, and in 1854, when he drew together all his hydrostatic coffee machines into one massive patent, it was registered in both France and England.

Loysel intended to exhibit at the Paris Exposition of 1855, and his designs covered a

2

complete range from a kitchen model, through a dining room percolator to catering sizes which were capable of serving two thousand cups an hour. The smaller machines had a long tube which was hand-filled with water, but the larger ones had longer and longer lengths of tube to provide the water pressure which is the basis of the hydraulic principle and required increasingly complicated arrangements of pipework, valves and stopcocks.

A stove at the base of the machine created steam pressure, but Loysel was always careful to emphasise that this was only to raise the water and not force it through the grounds as this was always done by hydrostatic pressure. There were double versions to be used in tandem and since greater capacity required greater quantities of ground coffee, multiple filters served by perforated tubes.

Machines of such size were really better employed making extracts from sugar beet, hops and malt but the one erected at the 1855 Exposition drew large crowds and brought Loysel a great deal of publicity.

The dining room hydrostatic coffee-machine can still be found today. Examples made by Shaw and Fisher of Sheffield in copper or Britannia metal will have inside a badge with the stamp of the manufacturer, the description 'Loysel Patent' and a facsimile of Loysel's signature. The lid is used upside down as a funnel to pour the water down the tube, but later models may have a separate dish and then the lid is merely a lid. They are extremely attractive mid-Victorian coffee-makers and survived in the catalogues of stores and ironmongers for many years. There was even a hydrostatic teapot.

3

1855 was the peak of Loysel's career. He lectured on his hydrostatic machines to the Institution of Civil Engineers in London and was elected an Associate, then he seems to have spent the next few years in Paris, living in the rue du Faubourg Montmartre. When he returned to England in 1864 hydrostatics had been abandoned but not coffee makers. His final long series of drawings show that he had become converted to the combined glass and metal, two-tier machine which by this time was familiar everywhere.

In 1865, after spending more than twenty years inventing coffee makers, he died. His hydrostatic machine with the long external tube was revived from time to time, but never became really popular. Loysel de la Lantais, however, has managed to remain remembered for his one attractive machine and for his attractive name.

4

5

3 - "Le Café du Percolateur" in the Place du Palais-Royal in Paris. Parisians flocked in their thousands to see Loysel's giant hydrostatic coffee machine. c. 1857.

4 - Three Loysel percolators with lids in place. Last half of the nineteenth century. Left: 3-pint capacity. Made in silver plate by Shaw and Fisher of Sheffield. Centre: 6-pint capacity. Made by E F Griffiths & Co. of Birmingham. Right: 4-pint size in Britannia metal by Shaw and Fisher. Bramah Collection.

5 - The same percolators with filling dishes.

6 - Patent drawing of Loysel's hydrostatic percolator. The lid became a funnel, and the weight of boiling water in the column is sufficient to push it upwards from the base through the grounds. As the liquor is drawn off, it passes through the grounds for a second time.

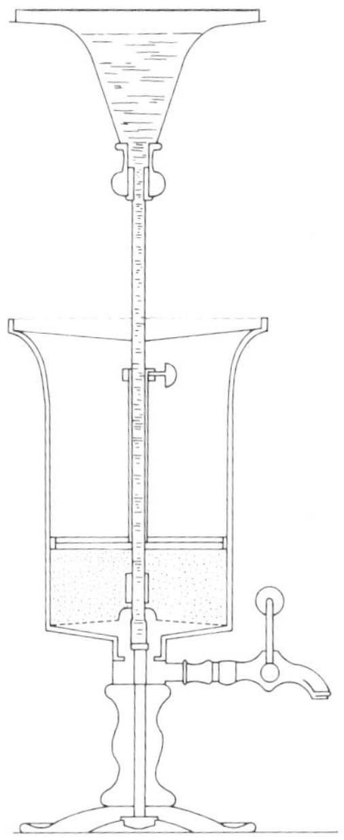

6

COFFEE MAKING IN AMERICA

1/2 - Two Pennsylvania coffee pots from the beginning of the nineteenth century. They were made of painted tin and in their plain and undecorated form were the cowboy pots which were kept simmering on fires in the old pioneering days.
The American Museum, Bath, England.

3/4 - Patent drawings of early American coffee makers. Even in the early twentieth century, American inventors were experimenting with concepts which had been familiar in Europe for generations.
Left: Percolator urn by G E Savage and J W Chapman, 1906. Right: Drip filter by W H Bruning, 1920.

John Smith, the founder of the Colony of Virginia in 1607, knew about coffee from his travels in Turkey, but there is no evidence that he took any to America with him. The Dutch, who settled Manhattan Island in 1624 may have brought in coffee during the next few years in the course of trade, but if they did it must have been small quantities and there is no mention of it. There is, however, a wooden mortar and pestle which was taken over on the 'Mayflower' in 1620 and was used much later to pulverise coffee.

The first person in the American colonies to sell coffee was Dorothy Jones of Boston who had a licence issued to her in 1670, but the first reference to anything like a regular coffee trade is in 1683 when William Penn of Pennsylvania bought supplies of green beans on the New York market for slightly under a pound a pound. Coffee houses appeared in Boston, New York and Philadelphia during the 1700s, but although the price dropped, coffee drinking was almost non-existent outside the major cities and in 1776, when the War of Independence began, such supplies as there were were seriously interrupted.

At this time, the principal sources of coffee were the Dutch East Indies, Arabia, Haiti and Jamaica and it was brought in by Dutch and British ships. In 1804 American ships started to import cargoes from the East Indies and the first coffee from Brazil arrived in Salem, Massachusetts in 1810. The vast Brazilian coffee industry was only in its infancy and total annual production in that year was less than 30,000 bags. By 1871 this had grown to over two million bags.

By the end of the eighteenth century an important difference was developing between the coffee trades of America and Europe. Capitals such as Amsterdam, London and New York all had coffee exchanges where the importers of green beans sold shipments and lots to the domestic markets, but in America influential firms of coffee roasters rapidly grew up in every large city making fortunes for a generation of men like Jabez Burns and Benjamin Green Arnold who were known as the 'coffee kings'. The large commercial roasting and grinding machines grew into factories and by 1845 it was said that there were enough facilities in and around New York alone to roast as much coffee as was consumed in the whole of Great Britain. Automatic packing was an inevitable extension and home roasting, which was still

1

2

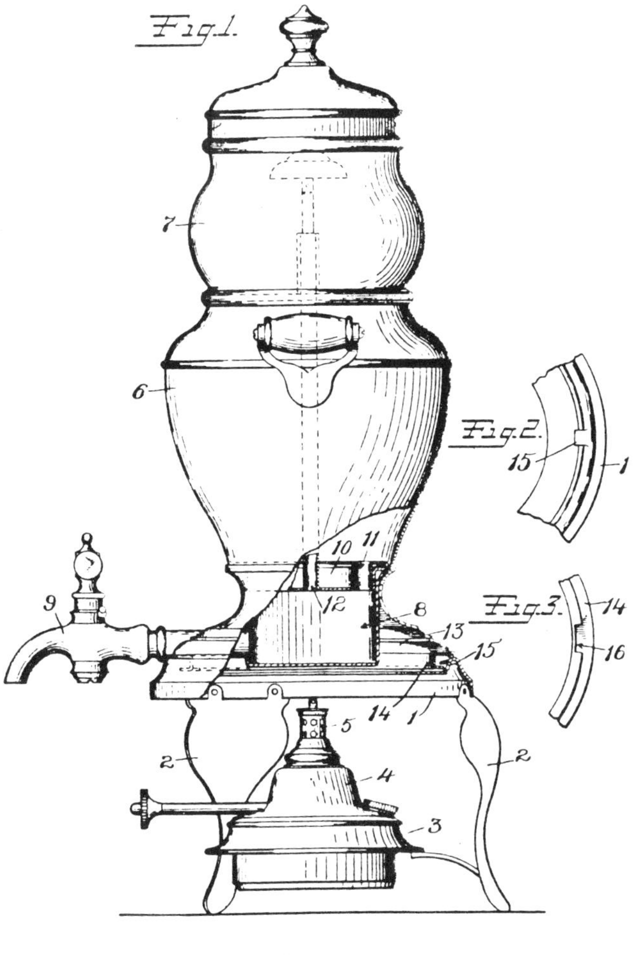
Fig.1.
7
6
Fig.2.
15
1
10
11
12
9
8
13
15
Fig.3.
14
16
14
1
5
2
2
4
3

3

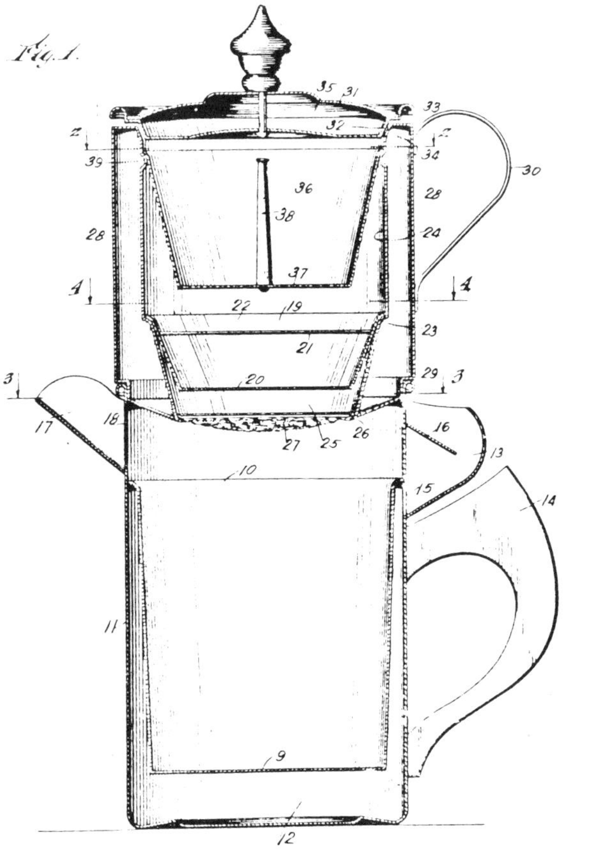
Fig.1.
35
31
33
32
30
34
39
36
38
28
28
28
24
37
4
4
22
19
23
21
3
20
29
3
17
18
16
27
25
26
13
10
15
14
11
9
12

4

common in Europe throughout the nineteenth century, virtually disappeared. Since this was where the money was to be made, invention tended to concentrate on this aspect of coffee making.

Rich, estabilished families used coffee pots of American silver and copper made in the European styles of the eighteenth century, but the millions of immigrants who arrived from Europe in the nineteenth century did not include coffee makers in their few possessions and lacked the means to buy them. The common practice was to boil coarsely ground coffee in a pan for fifteen minutes to half an hour on a stove or open fire. The 'cowboy pot', familiar from a multitude of western films, was the universal coffee-maker.

5

Because of the great distances between cities and settlements and the lack of communication, new and better methods could only spread slowly. Cookery books instructed the new generations of American housewives and tried to convert them to "coffee without boiling". They advised using a biggin, but even in 1844, *The Kitchen Directory and American Housewife* was telling readers to use a tablespoonful of ground coffee to a pint of boiling water and to boil it in a tin pot for twenty-five minutes -not longer or it would not taste fresh and lively.

At this time, coffee makers of great sophistication were proliferating in Europe, particularly in Paris and Vienna. They could only be afforded by the wealthy and middle classes, but even the less well-off had handsome copper, brass and Britannia metal pots and also quantities of good decorated chinaware available to them at reasonable prices because there was a large number of craftsmen to make them.

Craftsmanship requires money, traditional experience and volume. The pioneering society of America lacked all of these and also many of the materials. Coffee making had to be learned almost from the beginning.

6

7

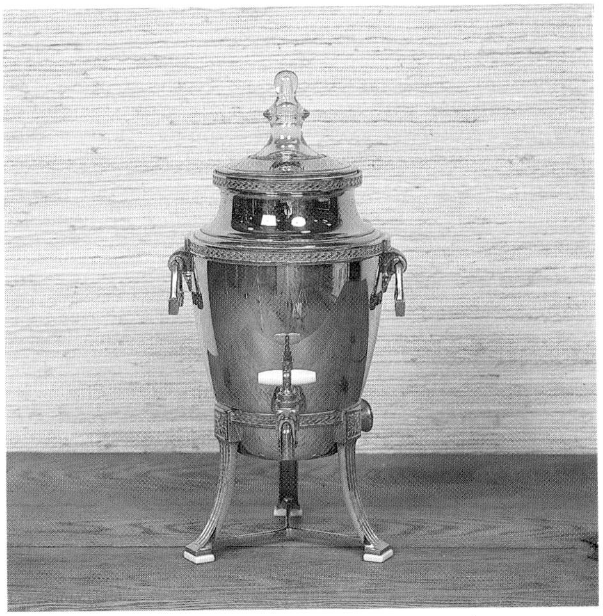

8

9

10

11

5 - This series of drawings of coffee machines is taken from Ukers' "All About Coffee" and summarises the most popular coffee makers in use in the nineteenth century in Europe and America. It was the search for examples of these machines which resulted, after twenty years, in the authors' collection.

6/11 - A selection of attractive American coffee makers. Photographs supplied by the John Conti Museum of Louisville, Kentucky, U.S.A.

There were drip filters in New Orleans, which had a large French population, but the coffee was not considered good unless it actually stained the cup. The first truly American style emerges with the Pennsylvania pots in enamel or lacquer with their highly individual decoration.

American semi-automatic coffee makers developed only slowly. They had condensers mounted on the top of the pot to collect the coffee steam and return the vital coffee essences back to the liquor where it was ruined by long boiling. The advice of Count Rumford had returned to his native land but was only partly understood. Typical of the mid-nineteenth century was the Old Dominion Coffee Pot in tin plate introduced by Waite and Senner in 1856. The *"Ladies' Home Magazine"* of the time described how this should be used: "If the coffee pot (The 'Old Dominion' of course, for in a common boiler this process would ruin the coffee by wasting the aroma) be set on the range or stove, or near the fire, so as to be kept hot all night preparatory to boiling in the morning, the beverage will be found in the morning, rich, mellow, and of a most delicious flavour.

"Coffee used at supper time should be placed on or near the fire immediately after dinner and kept hot or simmering - not boiling - all the afternoon."

12

12 - Two Universal coffee percolators by Landers, Frary and Clark of New Britain, Conn. First patented in 1894. One is in copper and the other nickel-plated. These were sold in large numbers in Britain. Bramah Collection.

It is truly amazing that so much trouble was taken to preserve the aroma and natural coffee essences when the brew itself was stewed to destruction.

From 1875 nickel-plating was being widely used and specialist manufacturers like Manning-Bowman had begun to appear. They adapted the French drip pot which in America was often called a biggin. It had a wooden block which pressed down the coffee grounds and extracted more liquor. This was inventing the hard way. It is difficult to understand why European experience was so completely ignored, but part of the answer must be the early American preference for very strong coffee. European coffee was considered too weak, and for a century, Americans visiting

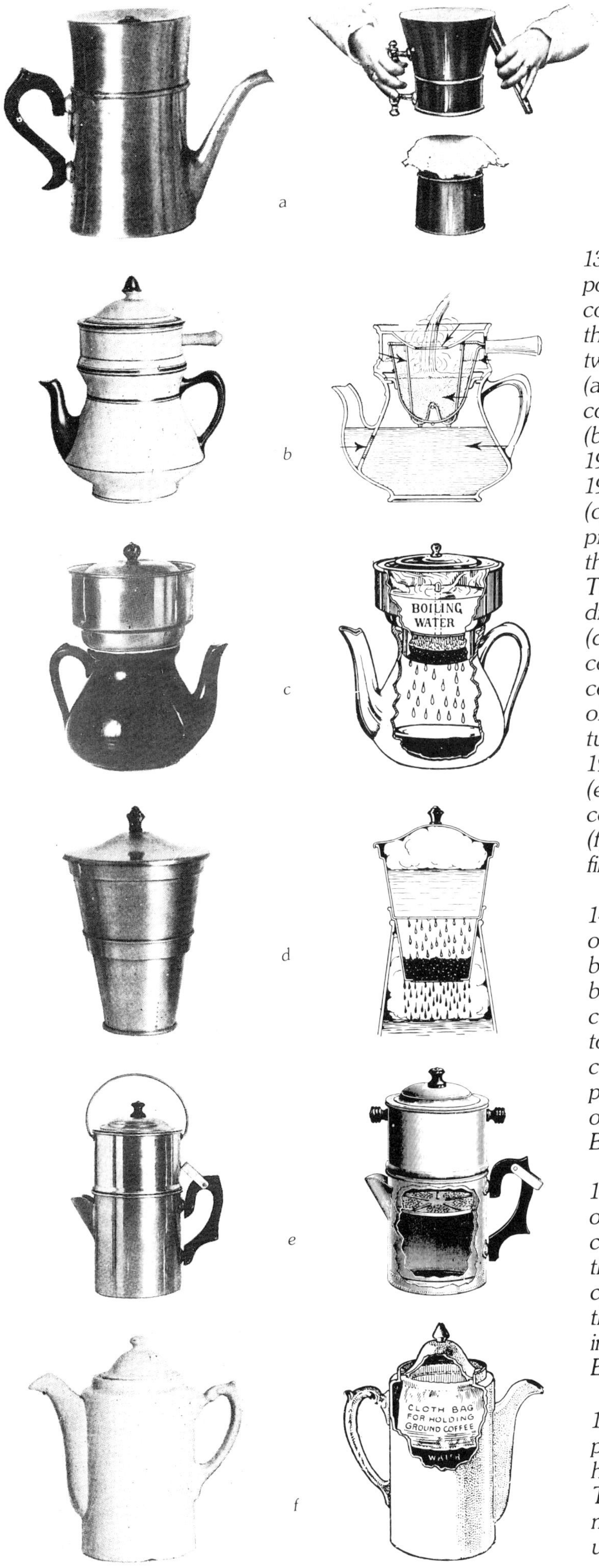

13

13 - A range of six popular American coffee-makers from the beginning of the twentieth century.
(a) Kin-Hee reversible coffee pot. 1900
(b) Tru-Bru Pot of 1911, improved in 1920.
(c) Tricolator of 1920, previously known as the Make-Right. This was a simple drip pot.
(d) Phylax adaptable coffee filter which could be put on top of any coffee pot and turn it into a drip pot. 1921.
(e) Galt Vacuum coffee pot. 1914.
(f) Blanke's cloth filter. 1909

14 - The Bencini pot of 1838. The coffee is boiled in the base, but there is a compartment at the top which acts as a condenser to preserve the aroma of the coffee. Bramah Collection.

15 - A copper version of the 'Old Dominion' coffee pot which was the classic American coffee-maker from the time it was invented in 1856. Bramah Collection.

16 - Aluminium percolator which was heated on a stove. This type of coffee maker was popular until quite recently.

14

15

16

Europe continued to express this opinion with some force. It was inevitable that they would develop what the French and Germans had been at such great pains to avoid - the pumping percolator.

This device did not mount its unwelcome invasion of Europe until the twentieth century, but there was a Manning-Bowman percolator in America in 1890. It sat on direct heat and had a central tube and glass cover and its main drawback was that it took a long time for the coffee to brew.

Even with a small water pocket in the base into which the tube was extended, this percolator would not begin to pump water in less than twenty minutes. When this started, the percolator could be safely left for whatever time was considered necessary to ruin the flavour. When electricity arrived, it greatly assisted this.

Although the pumping percolator had begun its seemingly unstoppable advance, another American coffee-maker was making its first appearance. According to the *House Furnishing Review* of January 1894, "What seems to be a perfect coffee machine on a small scale is the patent of an Englishman. It consists of a glass globe or boiler which hangs by means of trunnions from an ornamental stand, the

17

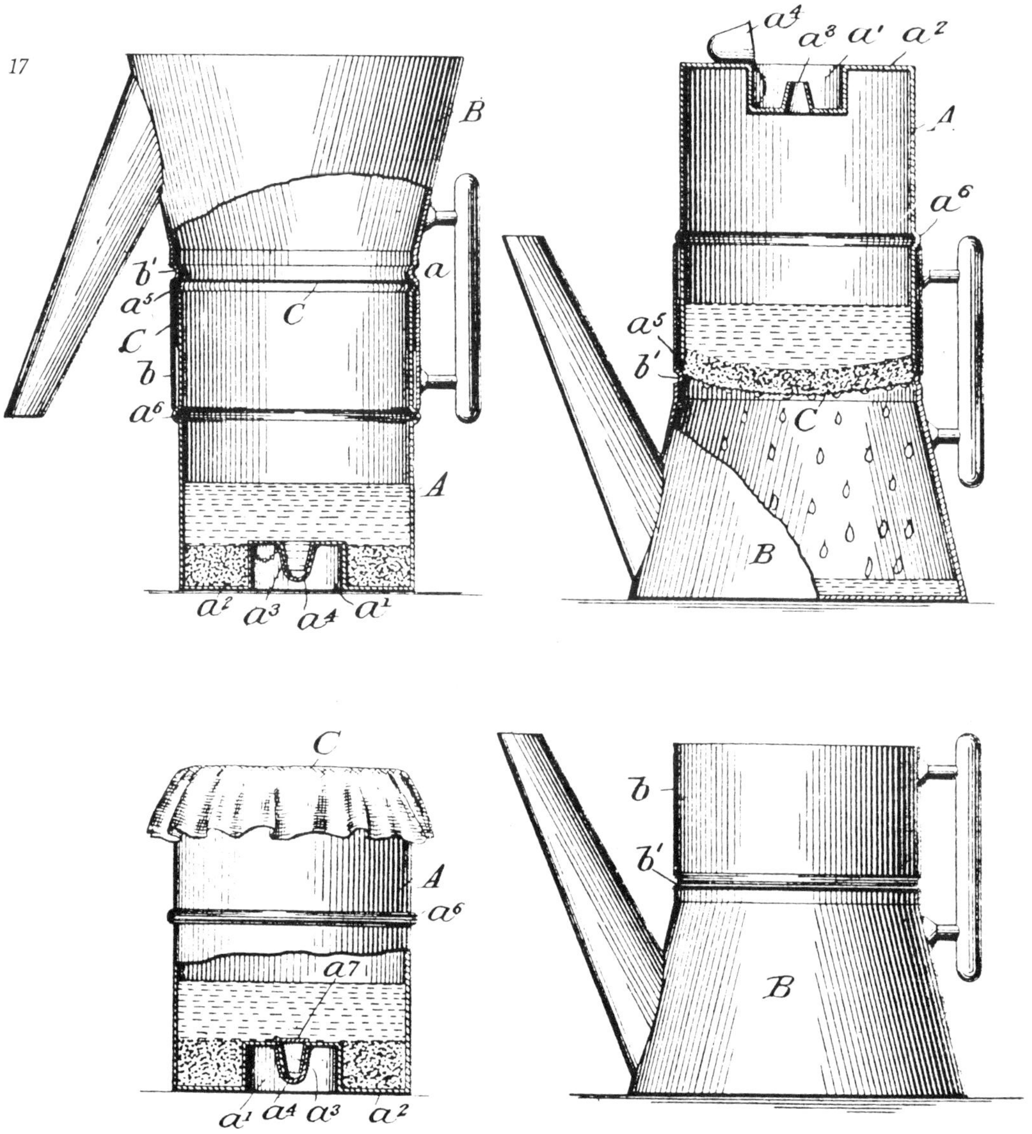

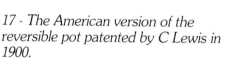

17 - The American version of the reversible pot patented by C Lewis in 1900.

The heavy style of drawing is much less attractive than delicate designs of seventy years previously.

base of which is a spirit lamp. A funnel-shaped vessel, terminating in a long glass tube, the junction being surrounded with a cork fitting the mouth of the boiler, forms the remaining portion of the appliance. This coffee-maker was neither new nor English. It was the double glass balloon cafetière of the 1840s.

The rights to it were acquired by two sisters living in Salem, Massachusetts. In 1909, one of them arranged for a heater to be made for the machine which she wanted to market under the name of 'Silex'. The flasks were to be made of the recently-developed 'Pyrex'. Enough time had passed for the glass coffee-maker to be rediscovered and relaunched as something fresh and modern. A new generation of coffee drinkers quickly accepted it as a typically American invention.

LATE NINETEENTH CENTURY AND EARLY TWENTIETH CENTURY DOMESTIC COFFEE MAKERS

During the whole of the time that coffee makers of greater and greater complexity were being developed, there was another method of brewing coffee which has to be mentioned with reluctance. This was cold water infusion, and it required the simplest of equipment. Generations of people made coffee in this way in the more rural parts of England and Continental Europe and it enjoyed a considerable popularity in America.

All that was needed was a bowl or pan, coffee grounds and cold water. The coffee was an ordinary grind and an ordinary roast, but more was needed than for hot water infusion. The cold water was poured onto the coffee and the mixture was left overnight or all day, strained and the liquor gently heated. The result was described by those who liked it as a mild, delicate liquor, low in acidity, but the chemical reactions of cold and boiling water with coffee are quite different. Modern coffee drinkers who have never encountered the method and probably do not even know it exists would say that, like instant coffee it produced something only distantly related to real coffee. Its virtue was, and indeed still is, its simplicity but for those who enjoy it for its flavour and prefer it to that of conventional coffee, there is now a modern and very complicated Japanese machine for making it.

Complication was the main characteristic of the coffee-makers of the last half of the nineteenth century. Existing models were given a more modern appearance and

1

2

1 - Italian pressure pot of the last quarter of the nineteenth century. Lavazza Collection.

2 - The Wika coffee machine which was popular in Germany and Austria in about 1900. This one is brass, although they were also made in a nickel-plated version. It has an inner container which dribbles cold water into the boiler to be heated gradually with the coffee grounds. When steam forms on the glass lid, the heat is removed.

3 nickel-plated. As patents ran out, they were appropriated by inventors all over Europe who added extra features to them and reintroduced them as new improvements, but the workmanship and complication which had once gone into decoration now went into mechanism.

It was not one of the best periods for style, fussiness being very much in fashion. The coffee-makers lost their original, care-free elegance and the additions made them more fallible, not more efficient.

There was a persistent interest in self-extinguishing devices, but these only worked if the machines were carefully used and properly cleaned, particularly those with a boiler which rose when the boiling water passed into the second chamber. People who were becoming accustomed to the efficiency and reliability of gas

4

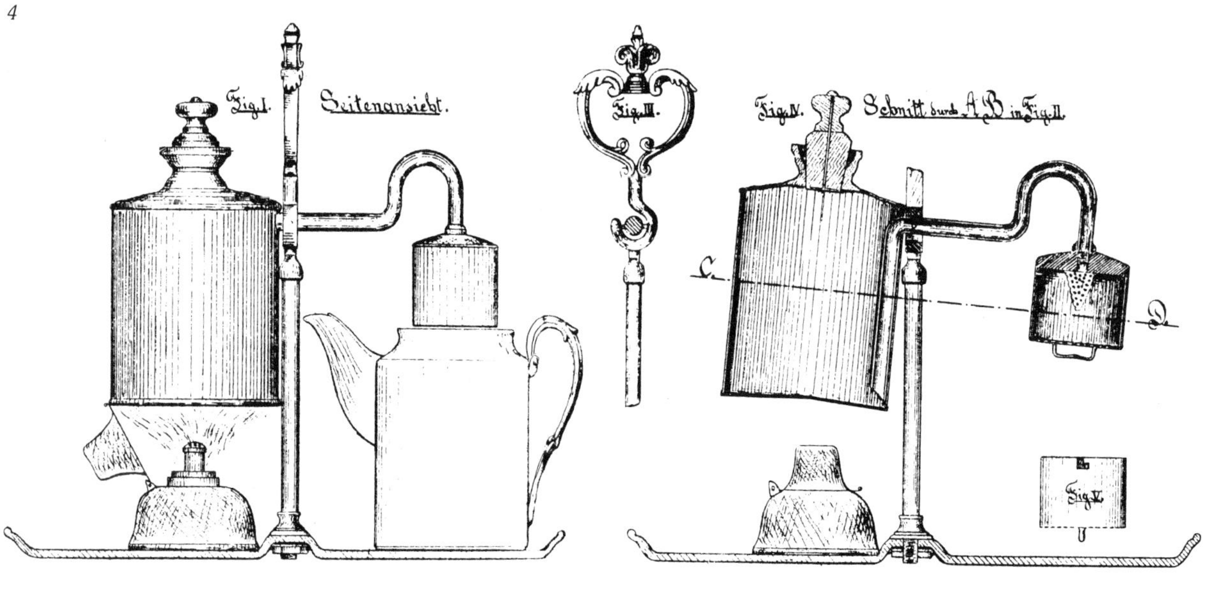

3/4 - Balancing pressure pot by Eicke of Berlin. 1878. It was easy to assemble and dismantle and was self-extinguishing. Any coffee jug could be used. Bramah Collection.

heating and lighting were less prepared to tolerate a machine which was not reliable and had no particular beauty to recommend it. Large numbers ended up as little heaps of scrap.

Inventing was now an international business. Patents were commonly taken out in several countries even though there was no intention of manufacturing there. It was merely a precautionary measure to prevent copying by competitors. There were also ideas which were never taken further than the drawing board. Success was beginning to depend on large-scale manufacture backed by advertising and a secure place in the price lists of hardware merchants and the new department stores, or in America the mail order catalogues which supplied a growing population who lived far from cities.

5

5 - The Caffeta in which the water and coffee grounds were heated together. When the water boiled the steam blew a whistle in the lid.
Bramah Collection.

6/7 - Swedish coffee makers. The water and coffee grounds were heated together in a glass flask resting in a depression on top of a stove. They were then encased in metal containers to keep hot.
Courtesy Robert Krasnai, Stockholm.

8 - 1892 version by Schauffler & Safft of the Vienna Incomparable. It has a tilting mechanism which automatically releases the lid of the heater and extinguishes the flame.

6

7

8

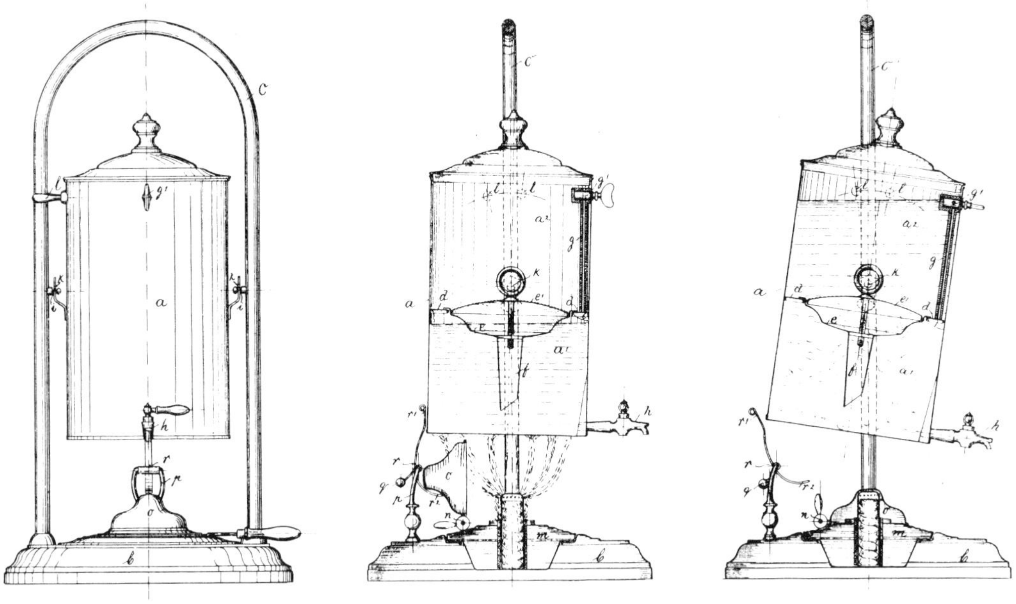

Few coffee-makers were actually improved. One was the reversible pot which was streamlined into an attractive oval shape and suspended on a stand over a spirit heater. It became popular all over Europe and America, known variously as the Potsdam boiler and the Russian egg-shaped pot. As the world became more industrialised and important people had bigger engines to occupy their attention, the various forms of drip pot consolidated them selves as the popular, classic way of making coffee.

One little coffee-maker which had no form of heating of its own was the plunger pot. This made coffee very much as tea was made in a teapot, but a strainer, the same diameter as the inside of the pot, was pushed down by a rod to separate the grounds from the liquor and hold them in the bottom of the pot. It proved to be immensely popular and has survived until today, going in and out of fashion, but never disappearing.

The universal coffee-maker of northern continental Europe was the 'Madame Bleu', a tall enamel pot with a strainer in the upper part. It was not always 'blue', but was made by the thousand in other colours and decorated with spots, stripes and flowers. Only a short time ago, pretty pots of this type were easy to find, but they are becoming scarcer.

Filter pots were also common in Italy, although there was also a market for percolators and pressure machines. The methods, and most of the inventors, came from outside Italy. The espresso machine

9

10

11

9 - 1910 advertisment for the Caffeta.

10 - Bavarian pressure pot which dispenses coffee through an outlet tube into a pot. Courtesy Ursula Becker Collection, Cologne.

11 - Two-handled spirit percolator with tap. English. 1930s.
Courtesy Ursula Becker Collection, Cologne.

12

12 - Two popular traditional Italian coffee pots. Left: the "napoletana" which was a version of the reversible pot which heated the water on a stove and then filtered it through the coffee when it was turned upside down. Right: The "milanese". Coffee was held in a strainer near the top and the body of the pot was filled with cold water up to the strainer.
When the water boiled it seethed through the coffee until it was judged to be strong enough. When the pot was removed from the heat, the liquor settled back, leaving the grounds behind. Fumagalli Collection, Milan.

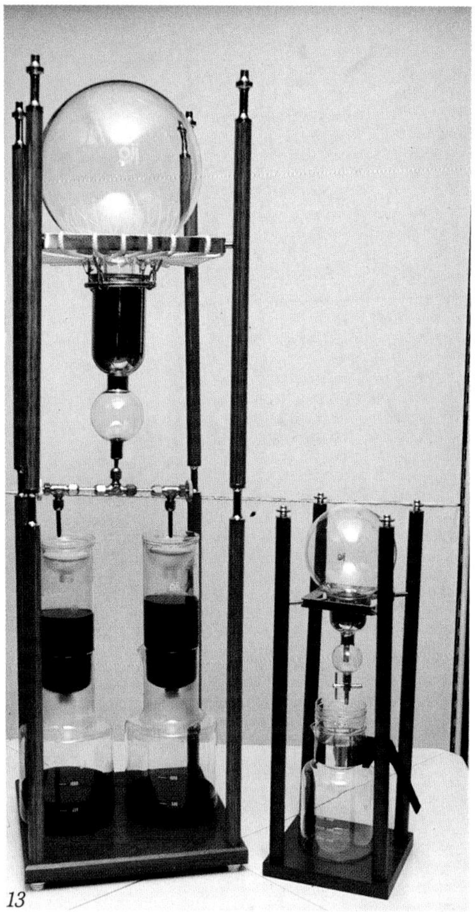
13

which was to be Italy's outstanding contribution to the history of coffee making, was still some years away.

14

German-speaking Europe also preferred the filter pot, but the more interesting development was the increasing social prominence of the coffee houses. In England, these had reached their peak of popularity at the time when the monarchy was being re-established and the first, organised financial institutions were starting to emerge. When businessmen moved into business premises, the coffee houses faded away. The literary figures who had congregated there began to notice that they were enduring a great deal of discomfort in order to drink coffee, which had never been regarded as of any great importance for its own sake. Men transferred their social life to clubs and coffee itself lost its popularity to tea.

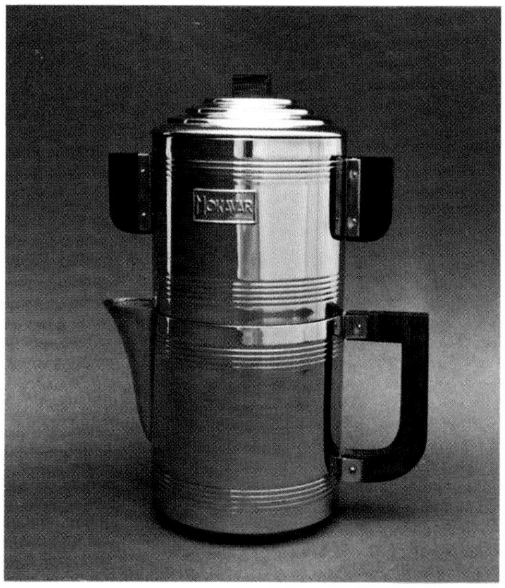

15

European cafés began as places of refreshment and established their reputations because of their comfort and service. They served generations of novelists, journalists, politicians and philosophers, enjoying particular prominence towards the end of the nineteenth century when new countries and new ideas were emerging.

16

13 - Cold water infusion apparatus from Japan in two sizes, height 85cms and 40cms. Courtesy International Coffee Organization, London.

14 - Madame Bleu. The most popular of all continental domestic coffee pots.

15 - The German Mokavar drip pot.

16 - Typical continental percolator jug which was heated on a stove.

17 A society which carried on most of its social life in cafés was not an English or American phenomenon, but it was well established in Europe and the number of cafés increased greatly when the railways began to move large numbers of people around in what was to become the tourist industry.

The new travelling public had their time confined by timetables and had to be supplied with refreshments in a hurry and at all times of the day and night. Urns, which were the traditional way of providing coffee in large quantities, could no longer cope with such numbers in spite of the improvements which were made to them and a completely new class of coffee-making equipment began to be developed by specialist manufacturers. This new equipment soon needed a new source of power, and the power, of course, was electricity.

17 - The most attractive of all reversible drip pots known as Potsdam boiler or Russian egg-shaped pots. Both of these were made in Paris. Bramah Collection.

18 - English copper coffee makers which worked in the same way as the double glass machines of the 1840s.
18 *Bramah Collection.*

THE COFFEE-MAKING GIANTS

Catering for large numbers has always presented special problems. The public has always recognised this, even when it has been most exasperated at what it was getting. The result has been a kind of armed truce. People did not really expect the coffee they were used to at home unless they were paying a high price for it, but at the same time they traditionally campaigned for something better. The sheer diversity of methods of brewing coffee at home ensured that while it was something that caterers were obliged to provide, they had very little hope of pleasing everybody.

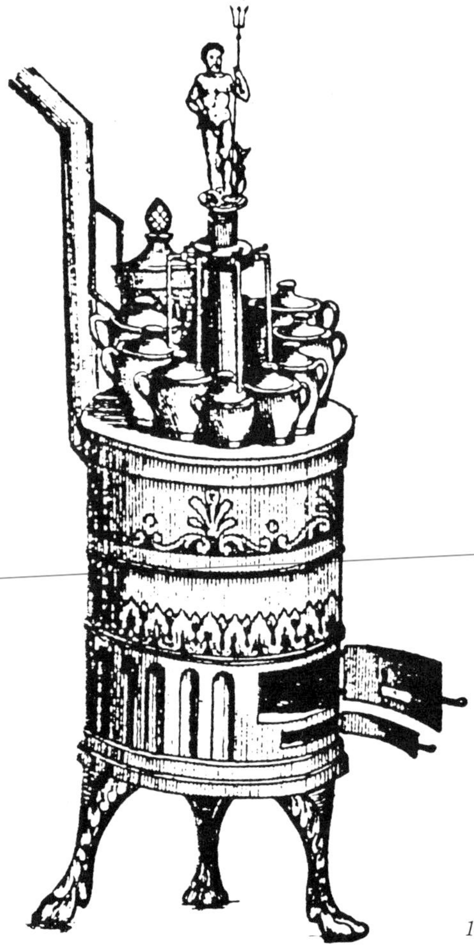

1 - *An early attempt at providing continuous supplies of coffee. Dingler's German patent of 1815.*

For the first hundred-and-fifty years after coffee first came to Europe, it was usually boiled or at least infused with the loose grounds in a coffee pot. Large quantities were made in bigger vessels such as cauldrons over stoves or open fires and then decanted into coffee pots. No better way was available until the first years of the nineteenth century when steam pressure was understood among a wide enough public.

An early attempt was the Dingler boiler of 1815, a German invention which looks startlingly efficient for its age. It is an extremely pleasing design because a great deal of thought has gone into the outer appearance as well as the inner workings. Steam pressure was built up in the boiler and then released through a carousel of valves and tubes into a series of coffee pots charged with hot water and coffee grounds.

The steam topped up the heat and agitated the mixture. It was similar to the steam injection device in coffee bars which heats milk and makes it froth. Steam injection is a good and reliable method of generating the steam and a sophisticated means of controlling it and the Dingler invention was really a long way ahead of its time.

Most of the mid-nineteenth century coffee makers designed for domestic use were incapable of providing coffee in quantity. The double glass flask cafetières and balancing syphons could not be scaled up. Large households and restaurants used either a variety of urn or a big drip pot, but these were not sufficiently versatile to supply the demands of the new travelling public which required refreshments to be continually available at all hours of the day or night.

2 - Portuguese gas-heated urn for making coffee. The casing is brass and the coffee is held in a ceramic container surrounded by water. Marked LISBOA Naohámelhor cafe que od a Pernambucana. Bramah Collection.

3 - Copper coffee-maker in which boiling water was forced by pressure through a central tube and through the coffee to fall back into the base. Height 60cms. The badge states that it was used by the Mecca chain of cafés in England. c. 1910. Bramah Collection.

3

2

4

4 - Two examples of coffee-makers familiar all over France in the early twentieth century. Bramah Collection.

5 - A French Reneka coffee machine from the 1920s. It is extremely heavy, wall-mounted and electrically heated and operates by a complicated step-by-step mechanism involving counterweights, stopcocks and circuit breakers. The coffee is eventually brewed in the ceramic pot which swings out on a hinge. Bramah Collection.

The Loysel hydrostatic percolator of 1854 was a serious attempt to provide a range of catering machines which were capable of supplying any demand up to thousands of cups an hour. The mechanical principles were perfectly sound, but Loysel was a civil engineer and unfortunately his machines really needed a trained engineer to operate them. Hydraulic power was slow and cumbersome, and gas was becoming more and more available in the cities and towns of Europe.

Gas was a form of heating which took up little space. There was no need for stoves or spirit lamps, no time taken up lighting fires or braziers and the heat was easy to control. It was, in fact, more suitable for supplying heat to a large coffee machine in a permanent position than to a small one which needed to be moved from room to room.

At first, gas heating was applied to what was already familiar. Gas urns replaced spirit lamps and stove-heated urns, but eventually the convenience of a gas pipe and the reliability of a steady and controllable gas supply enabled inventors, who were now increasingly also catering equipment manufacturers, to do some radical rethinking on automatic coffee machines for continuous supplies of coffee. Steam could be properly harnessed as it had been into engines for industry.

The age of mass catering followed the growth of the

5

railways. From 1850 large numbers of people were on the move and needed refreshments so it was only in the last half of the nineteenth century that café sets began to appear. Summerling brought out a series of improvements to existing British coffee machines, but in 1890 the catering coffee machine with the double urn supported by a central standard appeared which was to supersede them all and become the standard equipment in cafés and refreshment rooms everywhere. When electricity banished for good the stoves and charcoal fires, new and more efficient ways of harnessing steam were designed into machines which, essentially, were means of continuously supplying quantities of hot water on demand. It had been realised that if boiling water is constantly available the coffee can be brewed in whatever size of pot is most convenient.

The way that water was fed through the coffee grounds under steam or manual pressure now became something that was on the outside rather than the inside of the machine. The central supply of water could be tapped at several points.

On both sides of the Atlantic, catering coffee machines were made in brass and copper, stainless steel and nickel plate. Instead of being concealed in the kitchens of coffee houses, restaurants and refreshment bars, they were put on public view and were cased, chromed and burnished for the maximum visual effect. The new ways of using catering machines so that they produced freshly-brewed coffee meant that they had to be more conveniently placed on the bar counter and they became part of the decor of the establishments.

6

6 - Brass urn heated by gas for the English market. Late nineteenth century. Bramah Collection.

7 - Charles John Jones and William Mudd Still took out their first patent for this type of machine in 1902.

8 - Roma coffee maker. It has a light, modern look because of its uncluttered lines, but the fittings which serve the coffee are extremely heavy castings. Bramah Collection.

7

8

9 - German WMF coffee machine. 1927. Steam pressure forces water and steam through the coffee in the outlet on the left. On the right is a tube for heating milk by steam injection. Courtesy of the WMF Company, Germany.

10 - Large capacity percolator with milk heater. Courtesy Arnold Gould Trading Company Ltd.

11 - Modern WMF 'Filtromat' coffee machine from Germany. This is an example of a modern café machine providing hot water, coffee and steam injector. Courtesy WMF Company.

9

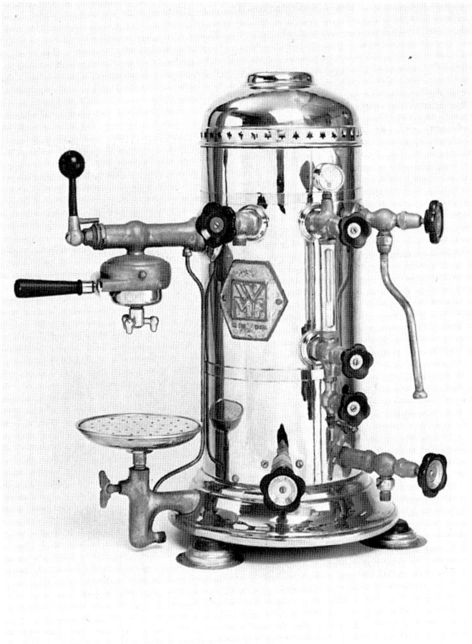

10

11

THE ELECTRIC COFFEE-MAKERS

The first electric coffee-maker was invented long before the general public had the means of making use of it. In 1881, Gustav Pfannkuche and Robert Dunston, working in London on improvements in electrical resistances, fitted an urn with a heating element comprising coils of wire embedded in plaster of Paris and covered by metal casing. It was at least twenty-five years ahead of its time.

Electric coffee-makers began in earnest in the early 1900s when heating elements were fitted to existing models. One of the two sisters who owned the American 'Silex' machine approached a company which manufactured heating appliances under the 'Torrid' brand. She asked them to make a small electrical stove or heated base for the double-flask machine which was now made in toughened 'Pyrex' glass. The owners of 'Torrid' products were so impressed with the 'Silex' that they offered to help sell it. It was primarily a domestic machine but thousands of them were sold to hotels and sandwich bars and having them on show in daily use was very valuable in creating public confidence in their safety. 'Silex' was later followed by 'Cona' and 'Cory' who brought out similar models with both electric and spirit heaters.

1

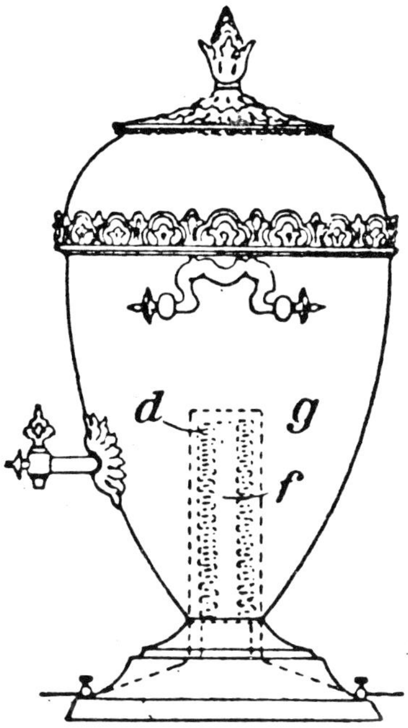

1 - Pfannkuche and Dunston's 1881 patent drawing of a coffee urn heated by an electric element - the first electric coffee maker.

2

2 - Femoka French electric pressure pot in which the water is forced by steam pressure up two external tubes and down through the coffee. The liquor is dispensed automatically into a separate coffee pot. Bramah Collection.

3

4

3/4 - Two electric percolators based on the American Manning-Bowman Universal. Courtesy Ursula Becker Collection, Cologne.

5 - Two double-cup pressure coffee dispensers. 'Veritas'. Made in France. Courtesy Ursula Becker Collection, Cologne.

6 - German combined glass and metal vacuum machine in which an element heated the water in the base and the coffee was brewed in the glass compartment at the top. The coffee was drawn back when the air in the base cooled to form a partial vacuum,

The other type of coffee-maker which benefited greatly from the new electric element was the percolator. Since 1890, Manning-Bowman had been manufacturing percolators which were heated on a stove or by a spirit lamp.

In their original form, they did not begin to pump water in less than twenty minutes, and neither did the improved ones of fifteen years later, fitted with an electric heating element. The solution was a slight change in the design. In 1908 Landers, Frary and Clark introduced its first electric 'Universal' percolator with a remarkable innovation which they called the 'cold water pump'. In ordinary electric percolators, then just beginning to be manufactured, the element had to heat all the water in the pot to nearly boiling point before it would begin to rise up the central tube. The Universal model had a small well or recess in the base around which the heating element was brazed. The heat was concentrated on a small quantity of water which started the 'perking' action in only two or three minutes. The cold water pumping percolators quickly outmoded all previous models.

The pumping percolator swept all before it because of the efficiency of the mechanism

5

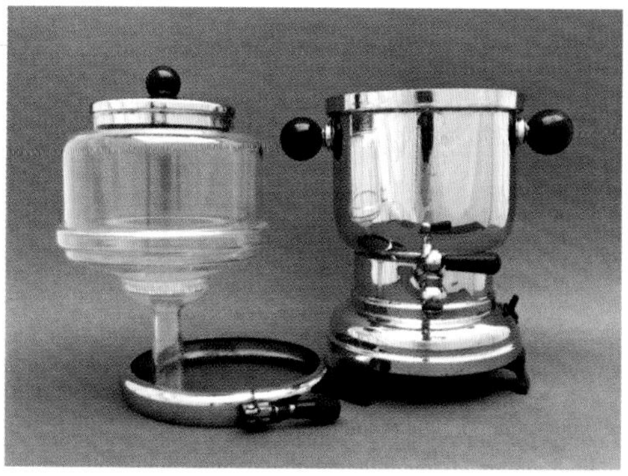

6

7

but the drawback was that it took a long time for the element to cool sufficiently. Similar coffee makers were also made in the United States in the 1930s. Bramah Collection.

7 - Hungarian machine from the 1930s. Heated water rises to mix with coffee in the top and a whistle blows to indicate that the power should be turned off. The liquor then returns to the bottom flask.
Urusula Becker Collection, Cologne.

8

and this advantage completely overwhelmed the very valid criticism that it ruined the coffee. The small quantities of hot water were sent up the central pipe to be sprayed over the basket of ground coffee in the top, filter through and be returned to the bottom to be heated again.

Almost immediately after the action started, what was being sent through in a continuous pumping cycle was progressively stronger and stronger coffee liquor which was being repeatedly boiled. This was quite acceptable to a large part of the American public which had been accustomed to boiling coffee and water together in a pan. Unfortunately the pumping percolator also invaded Europe, and the image of America as the source of all modern perfections was so overwhelming that the hard fight against stewed coffee which had been led so valiantly by the French seemed as if it might after all be lost.

8 - Left: French Paluxette. Centre: Italian Simerac. Both are pressure machines. The one on the right is an espresso with a hand-operated lever. Bramah Collection.

Electric pumping percolators were particularly popular among the British who had always found making coffee difficult and had largely abandoned the attempt. They had long ago obtained for themselves a constant supply of cheap, high-quality tea and were happy to leave coffee to foreigners. It was strange, but true, that the best and most expensive coffee beans came to Britain but in small amounts to be sold in high-class stores such as Harrods and Fortnum and Mason. Excellent coffee was served in the best hotels, but in general, English coffee was the worst in the world. It was not drunk to any great extent even among the middle classes, and even in the years just after the Second World War the most popular domestic coffee came in the bottles of 'Camp' coffee essence made by R. Paterson and Son of Glasgow. The percolator was perfectly acceptable to a public which had no strong opinions about coffee anyway. When instant coffee arrived in the scene after the war, the British took to it with enthusiasm as the solution to all their coffee problems.

Although continental Europeans had the greatest misgivings about them, percolators were manufactured, especially in Germany, in such profusion that it is possible to make a very interesting collection of them. The influence of America was so great and the complaints of American tourists in Europe so loud that for a long time coffee without boiling seemed doomed to extinction. It was saved partly by the new and powerful competition from the Italian espresso machine and also by a change of heart among Americans themselves who began to discover the merits of filtered coffee. While the electric percolator was gaining ground, it did, of course, have rivals. Most of the domestic coffee makers from the previous two generations were tried out with electric elements fitted to them. Electric urns, balancing syphons, and Vienna Incomparables appeared, enjoyed a brief revival and then vanished, this time for good.

9
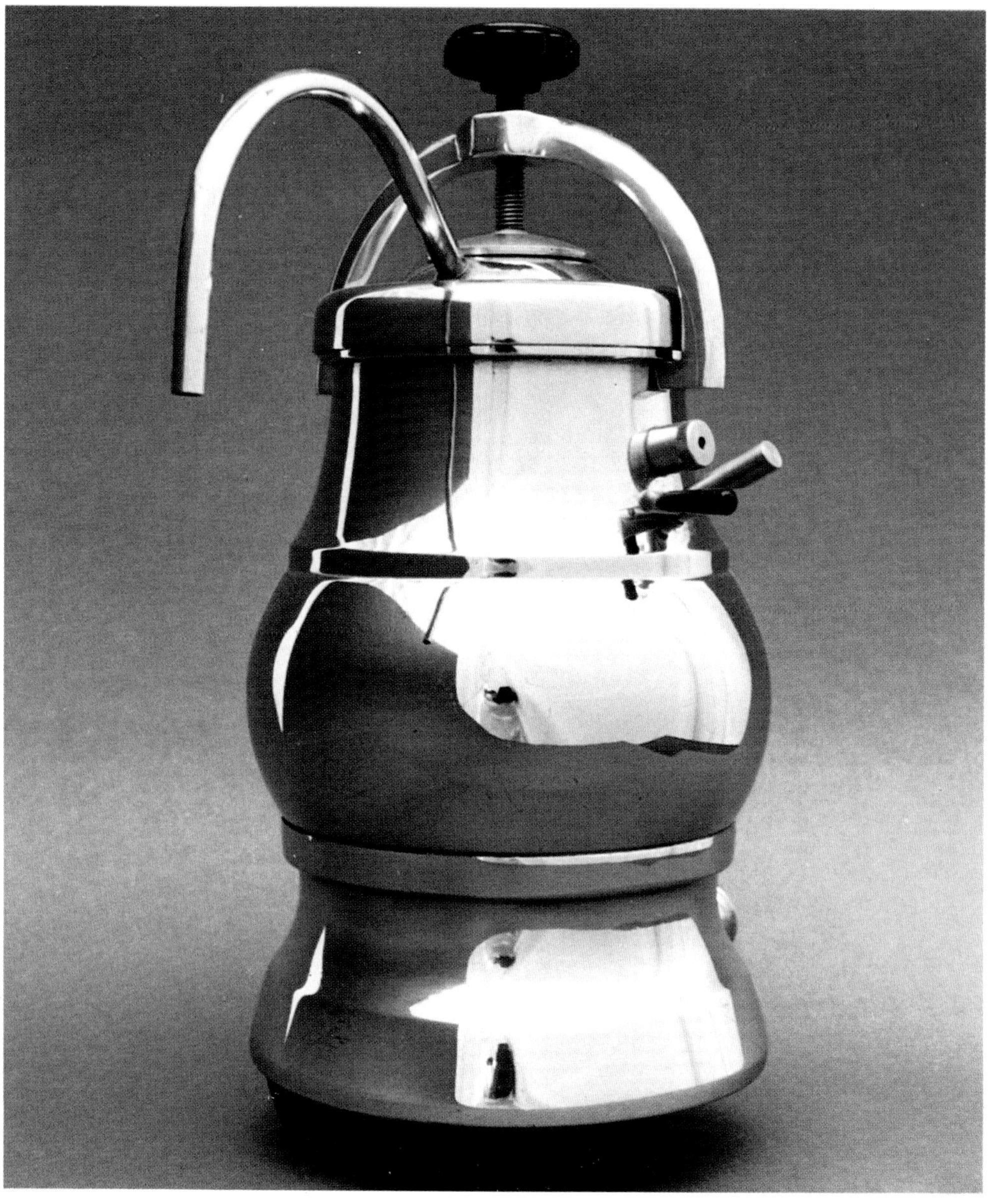

9 - Bavarian pressure pot which dispenses coffee through an outlet tube into a pot. Ursula Becker Collection, Cologne.

10

11

12

13

10 - Electric coffee-maker for use in cars. The grounds are kept separate by the sliding tin-plate mesh screen. Ursula Becker Collection, Cologne.

11 - 'Moccadur' electric percolator made in Berlin. The central tube has holes in the side of the upper section through which the boiled water flows onto the coffee. This machine has filter papers and is not a pumping percolator. The whole volume of water is sent up and over the coffee in one action. Ursula Becker Collection, Cologne.

12 - Hungarian 'Eta'. Pressure forces the water to the top through the coffee and back as liquor down the external tube and into the base. It was kept hot by the residual heat from the element. Ursula Becker Collection, Cologne.

13 - Vulcan two-cup pressure pot. German. Ursula Becker Collection, Cologne.

ITALIAN COFFEE MAKERS AND THE TRIUMPH OF THE ESPRESSO MACHINE

1 - "La Pavoni". A classic espresso machine manufactured in the 1920s and sold all over the world. Fumagalli Collection, Milan.

Coffee drinking began in Italy as early as 1600, but a characteristically Italian coffee maker did not emerge until the many small states had become a united country in 1860, with all the benefits of a single domestic market. Foreign inventions, in particular reversible pots and metal percolators and pressure pots, were copied or imported in considerable numbers because they made the strong coffee which appealed to the Italian taste. The first Italian patented machines could only add complications which were unnecessary and not widely adopted.

For generations, the two devices most popular with Italians were the "napoletana" and the "milanese". The "napoletana" was a reversible pot which was half boiler and half coffee pot. It sat on a stove until the water was boiled and was then tipped upside down for the water to drip through the coffee and then through a tube into a coffee pot.

Highly decorative coffee pots are disappointingly few for a country which has always had such an extraordinary artistic reputation, and delicately crafted machines seem to have been practically non-existent. The explanation for this may be the Italian artistic tradition itself. In Northern Europe, craftsmanship had channelled an enormous amount of talent into creating beautiful but quite humble domestic objects.
Italy was the home of Art. Why should a painter spend his time painting and gilding utensils when he could spread his talent over walls and ceilings? The Italians of the nineteenth century made their coffee in simple metal machines, but spent their money on pictures.

Among the first manufacturers to register an Italian patent was Giovanni Toselli, the architect who designed the Second Empire coffee-making toy locomotives in the 1860s. He was no longer playing with trains and had become a designer of commercial coffee machines in Paris. He and his competitors made serious attempts to invade the Italian market and they were joined by Italians with similar machines, but the designs were uninspiring. Something new was needed which would bring Italy to the attention of the coffee drinkers of the western world and in the 1890s that something new proved to be not an invention but a word, and the word was "espresso".

In the same way that "scherzo" and "sforzando" evoke for musicians a whole feeling, "espresso" for coffee lovers implied more than it

1

2

2 - Stand at the Milan Trade Fair in 1906. The Bezzera Company had been taken over by Pavoni who still used the name. The expression "Caffé-Espresso" was already in use. Photograph courtesy of the Italian Trade Centre, Bicester.

said. Foreigners easily picked up the implications of speed and the hint that they were being offered something special, and by the end of the nineteenth century the world was ready for a new way to regard coffee. People no longer stayed so much at home in their kitchens and dining rooms. They spent more time in cafés and travelling on trains, living lives which seemed to become faster every year. Espresso coffee, dark, Italian, exciting, suited this new modern way of life and was ready for a new generation of coffee machines to take advantage of it.

Catering for the public had required coffee machines which were simple for the staff to use and at the same time produced a consistently reliable drink. They were an unavoidable necessity and little attempt had been made to produce a thing of beauty. Loysel, in the Paris of 1855 had constructed a machine which was intended to amaze, and amaze it did, but it was the Italians who eventually acquired the reputation for creating something which was not only admired but loved.

British, American and German manufacturers of catering equipment were producing large capacity coffee makers by 1880 with stainless steel or chromium plated cases. They were as aesthetically pleasing as was possible for a mechanism whose prime consideration was efficiency, and they did their job very well. They had a central boiler and several outlet points for drawing off the water to make tea and coffee.
They were good, well-designed machines, but machines nonetheless. The Italian manufacturers, probably by instinct, added drama to the designs: what could not be concealed if it was to be convenient to the café owner, could be a positive advantage. The magnificent brass cylinders and fittings surmounted by the eagles

3

3. *Schneider 1930 model without a central boiler. Taps around the base controlled supplies of hot water to the individual outlets. Fumagalli Collection, Milan.*
4. *The "Eterna" machine also from the 1930s. The brilliant chromium finish covered a single large boiler. Gaggia Collection, Milan.*

4

with their spreading wings were intended not only to be seen but looked at. For the customer, buying a cup of coffee was to watch a dramatic performance. It was flattering to be able to sit and watch one's own individual supply of coffee grounds being clamped into the machine which would use all its hissing, steaming force to deliver one's own personal cup of coffee.
One of the first men who was instrumental in creating this new generation of Italian machines was Luigi Bezzera of Milan. He was an excellent engineer, but like many an inventor before and since, he ran out of capital. The mind of

5

6

an engineer, the personality of a salesman and the financial acumen of an accountant are a rare combination and in 1904 his company was taken over by Desiderio Pavoni whose coffee machines were then near the beginning of their long history.

Pavoni kept the Bezzera name and over the stand at the Milan Trade Fair in 1906 Bezzera and "Caffe-Espresso" are very visibly linked. All who liked espresso coffee were being inexorably guided towards this new style of Italian machine. The word not only meant a type of coffee but extended to the machine which produced it.

Pavoni's own "Ideale" model of 1906 could serve a hundred and fifty cups of coffee an hour. In 1909 "La Victoria Arduino", manufactured by Pier Teresio Arduino of Turin, improved this to a thousand cups an hour and by the 1920s, Italian steam pressure machines were firmly established all over Europe and had reached the United States. There was no doubt about their efficiency, but the coffee that they produced was too bitter even for some Italian palates and eventually the whole concept of coffee-brewing by steam pressure was made obsolete by Achille Gaggia who had become

7

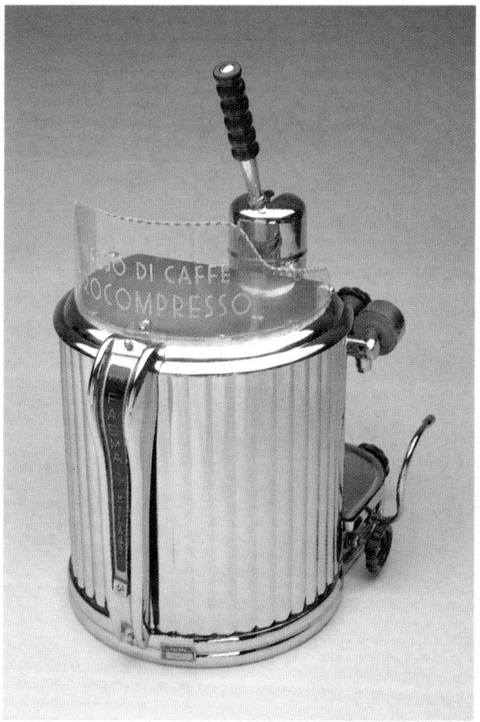
8

5. 1922 poster for the Victoria Arduino coffee machine. "Espresso coffee" was an expression which had been in use on the continent for more than twenty years. When a new generation of young British tourists was able to travel to Europe for the first time after the Second World War espresso coffee came to symbolise a totally new culture and, for many of them, their first serious experience of "real" coffee.

6 - San Marco coffee machine which supplied steam for a steam injector to heat milk, hot water for espresso coffee and an extra supply of hot water alone. It was another break from the traditional style of catering coffee machine.

7 - A Gaggia machine of 1948. The design is a complete break from the brass boilers and eagles and recalls the juke boxes of the same period.

8 - A Faema espresso machine of 1950 with a single handle and a similar modern design.

absorbed in the subject during the Second World War. In 1946 he designed and marketed in Italy the first true espresso machine "to work without steam", and these words actually appeared on the early models.

The chrome and gold finish on the front and sides of the Gaggia machine covered a specially plated heavy copper pressure boiler which rested on the top of the bar counter. pressure boiler which rests on the top of the bar counter. Inside, the water was heated to boiling point and controlled automatically at a pressure of 20 pounds per square inch. Fixed to the tank were cylinders containing pistons worked by powerful springs. A filter holder containing specially fine-ground coffee was clamped to the bottom of each cylinder. On top was a lever, rather like the English beer pump, which controlled the piston. When the lever was pulled down, water drawn from the bottom of the boiler (to exclude steam) flowed onto the coffee. When the lever was released, the spring drove the piston downwards, forcing the water through the coffee at a pressure of about 60 pounds per square inch, extracting all the good properties from the coffee.

In Italy the new espresso machines made by many manufacturers were quickly recognised as revolutionary and were soon selling through most of Europe and certainly led to the coffee bar craze in London in the 1950s where instead of trying to fit the espresso machine into the existing atmosphere of the snack bar with its stale sandwiches and three-day-old buns, it was decided to create a modern coffee bar around the machines.

The first one opened in Soho where there was a substantial foreign population to appreciate it, and it was an instant, sensational success. By 1960 there were over two thousand modern coffee bars in Britain, five hundred in London alone. The most interesting feature of the coffee bar phenomenon was that it owed practically nothing to the catering trade. The people who opened them were architects, antique dealers, wine merchants, interior decorators, sculptors, dentists and film stars. The fact that English caterers had refused to have anything to do with the espresso in its early days proved to be a good thing because the outsiders created a new and badly needed class of café with clean, modern décor and good coffee and food at reasonable prices.

The special importance of the espresso machines to the English market was that they made the general public aware of the success that the Italian commercial coffee machines had been establishing for two generations. The timing was fortunate. The Italian cinema, the motor scooter and the espresso coffee machine were all combining to create a new post-war image of Italy. However, even Gaggia machines were not to remain for long the last word in efficiency. His competitors picked up the ball and ran with it, if one may use an expression from rugby football. The pistons which were required to produce thousands of cups of coffee a day were subjected to a great deal of stress and wear and the Cimbali Company brought out a hydraulic system which superseded spring levers.

Faema was soon a prominent name among the firms which established a reputation for

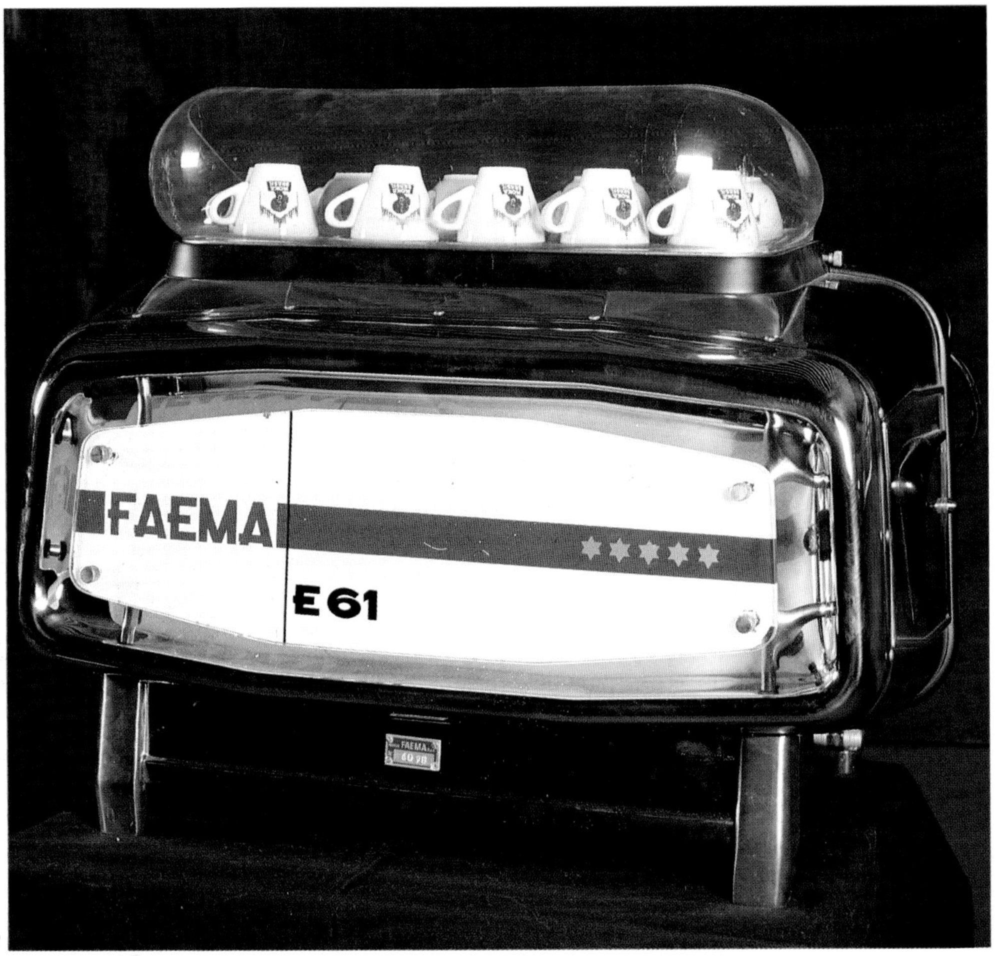

9

10

developing the modern espresso machine in the years following the Second World War. The basic design was capable of a great deal of improvement, both in efficiency and in the quality of the coffee, and Faema introduced a model which had as its main feature an "erogazione". The large reservoir of boiling water contained in a tank had never been entirely satisfactory since the coffee was made, as often as not, with stale water which spoiled the flavour and also furred the pipework of the

9 - A Faema espresso machine of 1961. There was no central boiler or large reservoir of hot water. Enough heated water was kept available for each individual outlet. The pump which dispensed the cup of coffee also drew into position another cupful of cold water to be heated in its turn.

10 - A Pavoni machine from 1956. At about this time the boiler, which had been a tall cylinder, started to be laid on its side to be incorporated into long, low espresso machines with serving points ranged horizontally instead of round a cylinder.

11 - Electronic machine of a modern conception: "La Cimbali".

12 - Brasilia machine of 1980. There is a boiler in the cabinet under the cups and the dome with the eagle on top is only for decoration.

13 - Modern Brasilia machine. The old nostalgic shape has been reproduced but modern methods of water heating have left space inside for storing cups.

11

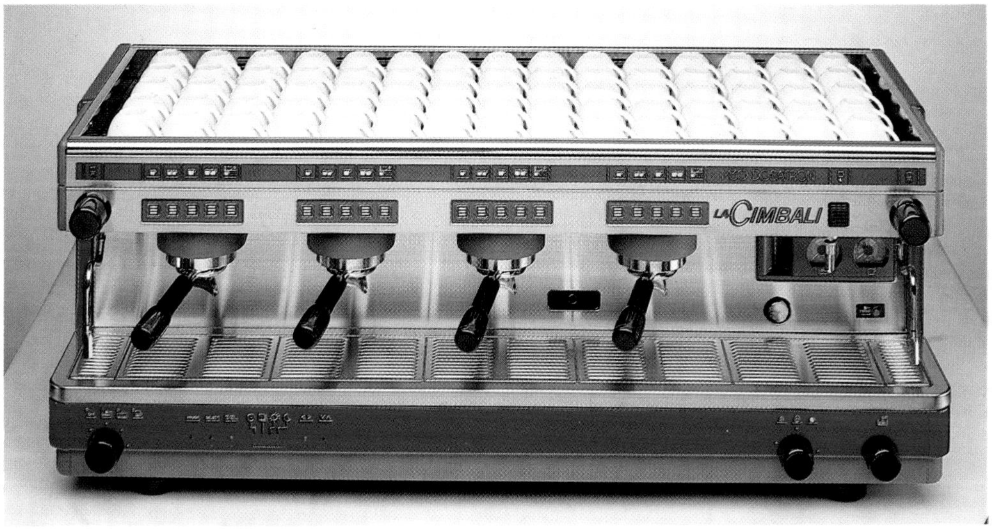

13

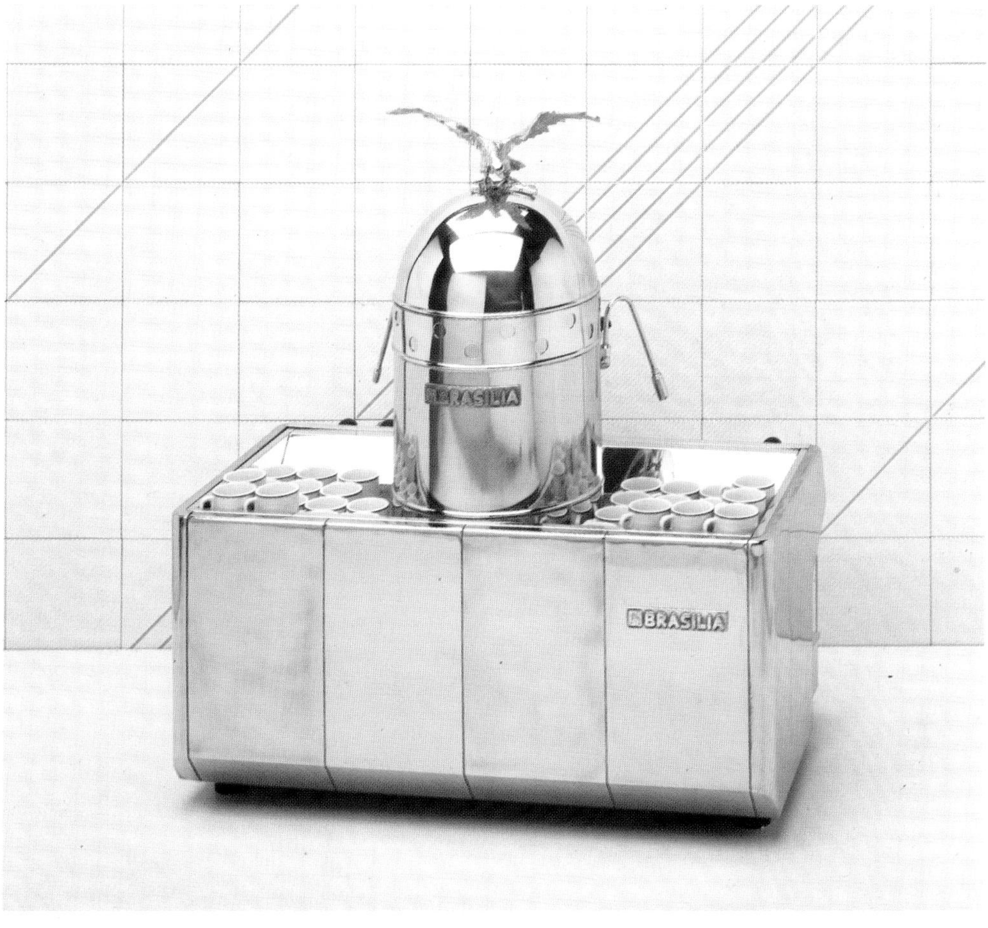

12

14

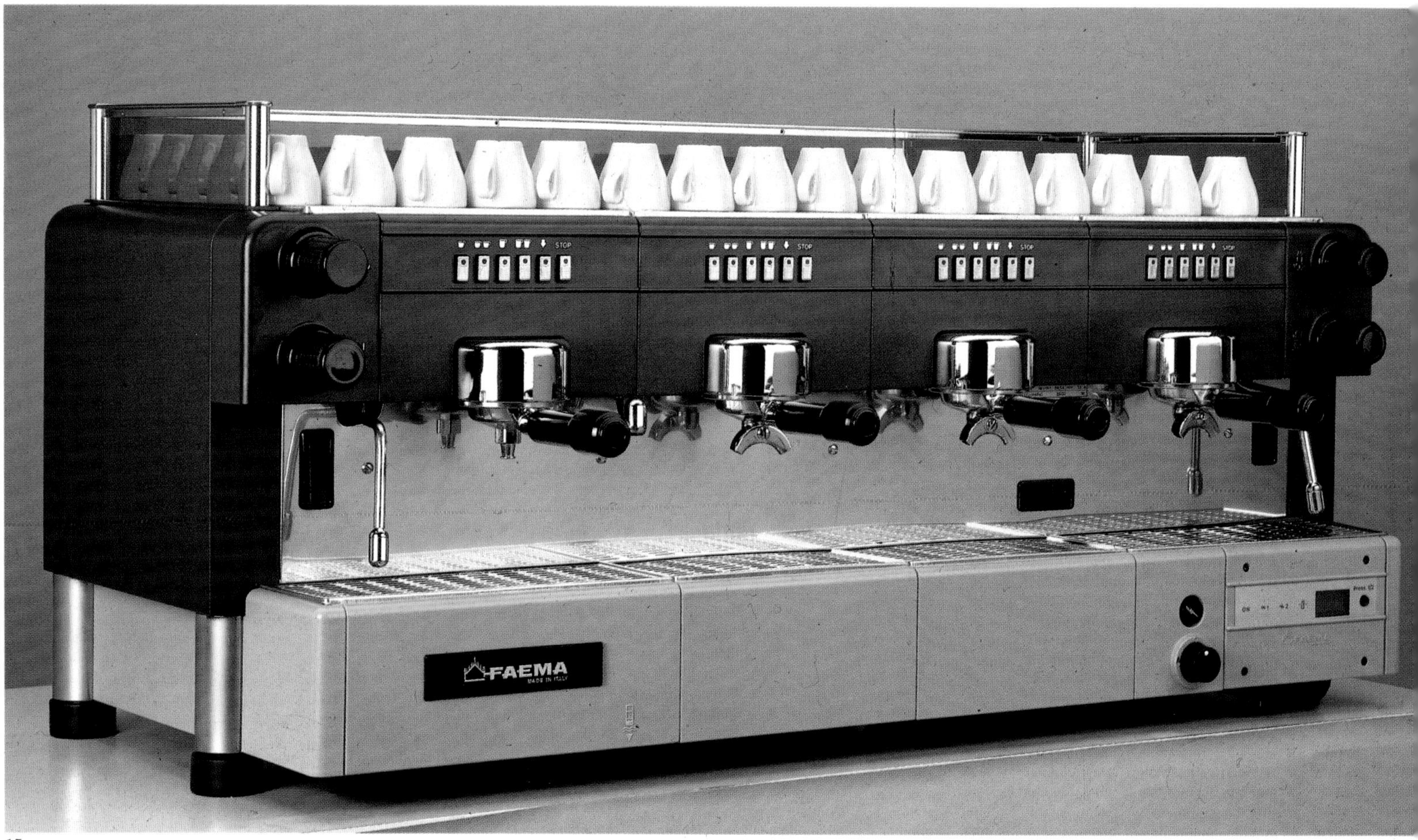

15

17

16

14/15 - As cafés and restaurants are fitted to ever-increasing standards of comfort, espresso machines are being redesigned with all the advantages of modern electronics and materials. These two models are manufactured by Faema of Milan. The top one is the "Special Lux" and the lower one is the "Tronic".

16 - The "Universal" of around 1920, an Italian pressure pot heated by electricity and capable of serving six small cups of coffee all at the same time. Fumagalli Collection.

17 - Two machines heated by alcohol, one in copper and the other in tin plate. They carry the trade marks "Cozzante" and "Aquilas" and date from the 1920s. Fumagalli Collection.

18 - Two domestic electric coffee makers, the "Neo Watt" of 1930 and the "Baby Lutetia", a four-cup machine of 1920 made in brass and nickel. Fumagalli Collection.

18

espresso machine with chemical deposits.

Faema used the water boiler to keep the working parts of the espresso machine hot but the water to make the coffee was only heated and drawn off in small quantities as required. Fresh water then replaced it in the pipe to be heated to the correct temperature within twenty-five seconds ready for more coffee. The copper

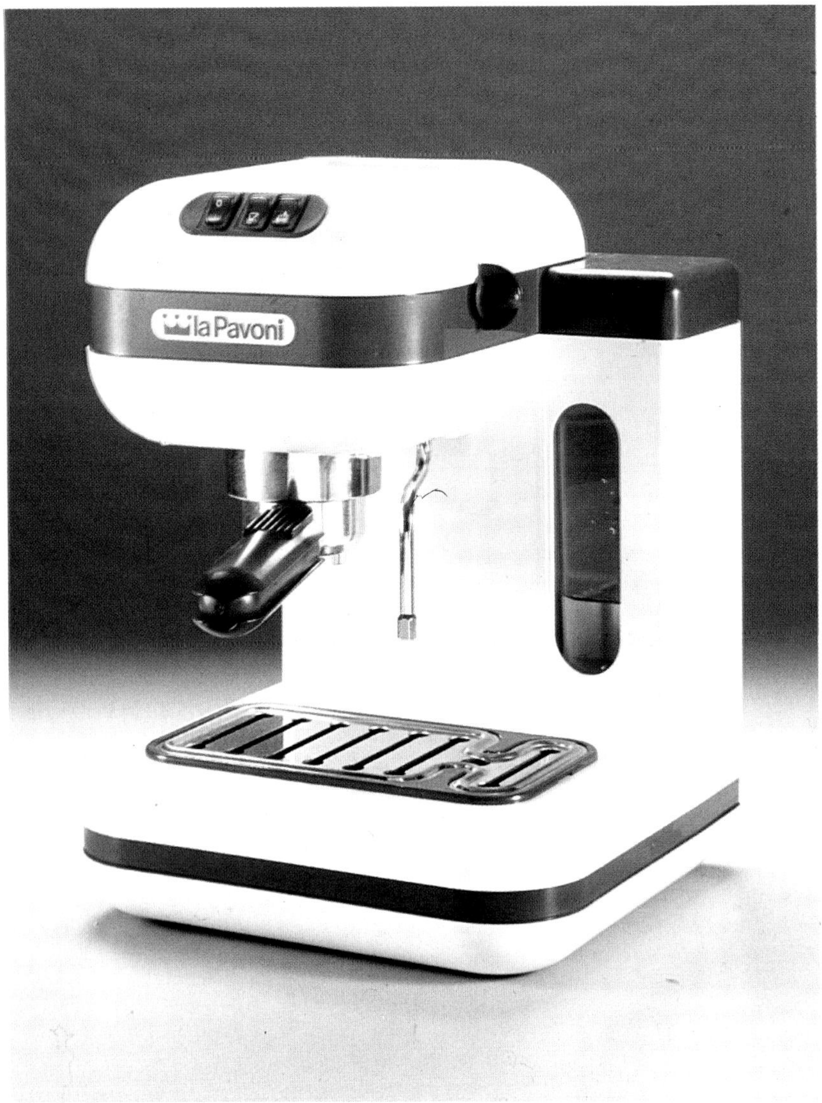

19

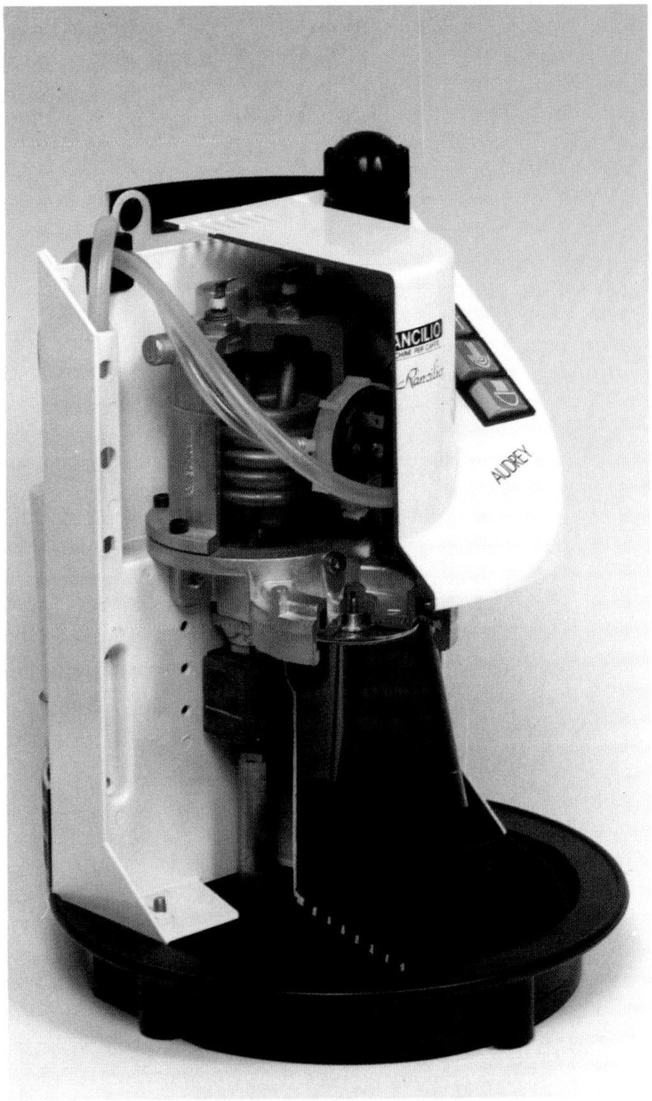

20

supply pipe was immersed in the boiler which acted as a water jacket.

Faema also incorporated a water treatment unit which "sweetened" the water by extracting the chemicals which furred the pipes and boiler and thus eliminated many servicing problems for both the café owner and the machine supplier.

The flavour of the coffee produced by the new generation of espresso machines was much improved. The temperature of the water, about 90°C, was just right, the good qualities of the ground coffee were completely extracted and the liquor produced had a thick, creamy texture with a characteristic all of its own.

The espresso machines manufactured for cafés and restaurants were expensive and solid examples of engineering, designed for hard

19 - One of the latest in their series of machines extending over nearly a century, Pavoni's domestic espresso with a plastic case and integral coffee grinder.

20 - The "Miss Rancilio". The casing has been cut away to reveal the interior.
The space which in a traditional coffee-maker used to be taken up by a container for boiling the water conceals the latest improvements in water heating, thermostat and electrical wiring.

21/22 - Two of the most up-to-date Bialetti domestic models, the "Cappuccino Super" and "Viva il Caffé".

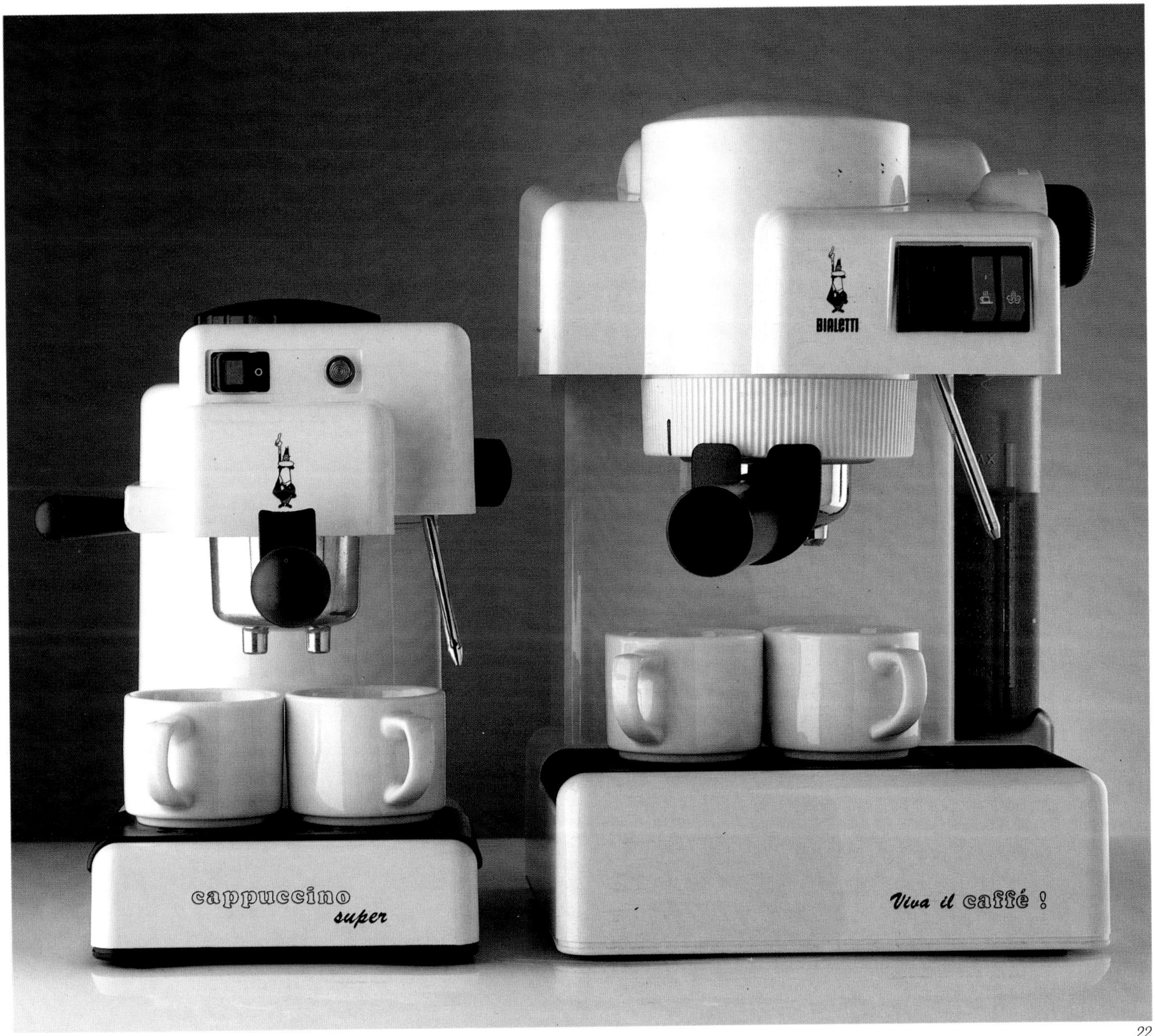

21

22

and continuous use, but the principles of their operation and technical advances were easily adapted to smaller, domestic coffee makers.

It was inevitable that people who enjoyed espresso coffee in restaurants would demand something similar at home and lighter-weight and smaller domestic versions which nevertheless used all the technology of their bigger commercial brothers were soon available with the characteristic clip-in filter holder.

The typical modern domestic espresso usually includes the Faema type of "erogazione". It consists of a small pump, a small boiler which keeps the water at a constant temperature by means of a thermostat, and a filter with the ground coffee clipped onto the pump. When the espresso is in operation, the pump transfers cold water to the boiler, forcing the hot water already there through the coffee.

The espresso method was

23

24

25

23 - A complete coffee-making kit. This machine incorporates an electric grinder which supplies the coffee absolutely fresh for the espresso machine beside it.

24 - The "Amica" cappuccino machine which automatically produces a cup of hot and frothy white coffee.

25 - "Ciao" another example of a compact and modern design which fits an espresso mechanism and steam injector for heating milk into the smallest possible space.

fundamentally different from nearly all previously mechanisms in domestic coffee makers in two important ways. It used easily controllable pressure — older pressure machines had worked in their own time rather than that of the person using them — and instead of dispensing a whole pot of coffee it supplied it a cup at a time. This gave the designers advantages of scale. It was no longer necessary to accommodate a jug and also a boiler of equivalent size. Domestic espressos could combine the interesting features of the commercial models and a range of modern styles and finishes.

These improvements, which all took place in the 1950s, enormously enhanced the international reputation of Italian coffee, yet within Italy tastes in coffee remained a very individual thing, varying from region to region. Coffee roasting has always been of great importance. In Northern Italy it stops when the beans are still brown, but farther south, away from the influence of France and Austria which played such a large part in Italian history, the beans may be roasted until they are almost burnt. Travellers will also notice that the cups become smaller. In Naples a cup of coffee is hardly more than a drop, but however it is prepared, coffee is a drink which in Italy is taken very, very seriously.

COMMERCIAL FILTER MACHINES

The most recent important event in the history of the coffee trade has undoubtedly been the post-war development in Britain and America of an enormous consumption of instant coffee. It owed its success to massive advertising on television and for a long time was a serious threat to the existing markets in ground coffee. However, two developments have tended to draw the two branches of the trade closer together. The first was the constant improvement in the quality and flavour of instant coffee and the second was the packing of freshly roasted and ground coffee in sealed plastic packets. With a great new increase in prosperity, there were millions of households where instant coffee and freshly-brewed real coffee existed side by side. Through instant coffee, a new market for 'real' coffee was actually created, but it was necessary to have all the uncertainties removed from brewing it.

The public not only wanted a better quality coffee to drink at home but at its place of work too. In factories and large offices, the only alternative to mass catering in company canteens or morning and afternoon supplies of coffee and tea wheeled round on a trolley (a peculiarly British custom) was the vending machine.

Hot drink vending started in the 1950s in the United States and soon spread to Europe. The quality of the drinks from the early machines was not very impressive, but it improved as the machines improved and the coffee companies manufactured powdered ingredients which were more suitable to this type of mechanism. The problems were overcome and vending machines have survived and become accepted because there was an overwhelming need for them. There was also a new, growing place for small, reliable, easily-operated coffee-makers which could be used in individual offices and workshops to supply coffee while people were working and whenever they wanted it.

When Americans began to be disillusioned with the percolator and looked around for a better method of making coffee, all the new technology was in favour of a filter machine. The principle itself had been demonstrated beyond all doubt for centuries, but what was necessary was for commercial coffee machine manufacturers to bring together everything that had been learned and combine it into something that was as easy to use as an automatic washing machine. The public was accustomed to domestic appliances that were trouble-

1

1 - An early Bunn commercial coffee filter from the 1960s. Bunn was one of the early companies which put filter machines serving fresh coffee into American offices to compete with vending machines. Courtesy John Conti Museum.

2/5 - A group of automatic filter machines intended for cafés and offices which introduced a new British public to filtered coffee from the 1960s onwards.

free, efficient and could be used without having to be understood. They would accept nothing less in a coffee-maker and there was a long history of obsolete and abandoned coffee makers to prove it.

It was absolutely vital that there should be improvements in the way in which the coffee was filtered. Ever since the infusion bag and drip pot, all coffee machines had some form of cloth strainer, metal mesh or perforated container to separate the grounds from the coffee. The quality of the brew depended on whoever made the coffee using the appropriate roast and grind and this was left to individual judgement. Almost always some grounds got through into the liquor. The simple solution to this was the modern disposable filter paper, which we owe to Frau Melitta Benz.

As early as 1782, Dr. J. G. Krunitz had recommended putting blotting paper into a sheet-metal, tin-coated funnel, adding ground coffee and pouring boiling water in slowly.

Frau Benz was a German housewife who had a great deal of practical experience of making coffee. She tried linen towels and also blotting paper as strainers but found the ideal solution in strong, porous paper. Thus came about the first commercially produced filter papers. By 1912 her husband was selling thousands of metal pots with paper filters through the company that he named Melitta. Over the years, filters were folded and adapted into the shape of the filter funnel. Coffee companies and filter manufacturers made their products compatible to each other and to filter machines.

Modern, electrically-operated filter machines date from the early 1960s and they were first developed for commercial use

Still
Kenco
Kencomatic

2

3

BRAVILOR - mondo
electronic
BRAVILOR

4

BRAMAH
INSTRUCTIONS FOR COFFEE MAKING
BRAMAH
BRAMAH

5

as in their early days they were solid, heavy, rather large and expensive to make. A great deal of experiment and experience (which is not necessarily the same thing) went into them before they evolved into the neat, modern domestic filter.

The first problem of the filter machine was one of size. It had to be twice as large as the amount of coffee it produced since the same amount of fluid had to be accommodated in two places. Early filters heated the water in one compartment and then returned it into another as coffee. Electrically-heated commercial filters with stainless-steel cases dispensed the liquor into glass flasks. Where the boiler and element went had to be determined by trial and error.

6

6 - The simple mechanics behind a modern automatic filter machine fitted with a flow boiler. Water poured into the upper tank starts to flow through the silicon tube into a boiler around which is wrapped an element. As the water reaches boiling point it is forced up in small amounts through the metal tube and onto the coffee at slightly below boiling temperature.
Courtesy Coffilta Coffee Services Ltd., Southampton.

The earliest electric filters had a reservoir tank filled with water which was heated by an immersion heater and kept at the correct temperature by a thermostat. To make the coffee, a quantity of cold water was poured in to displace part of the heated water through a tube and over the coffee grounds held in a filter to drip through into a flask. The disadvantage was that since there was always water in the machine, it would often be stale and always first thing in the morning when fresh coffee is most appreciated. By 1968 this method was improved when fresh cold water was heated by an aluminium heat block in the top of the machine. The water passed through holes in the heat block and then onto the coffee, but there were other ways of achieving the same result. One was to use a more powerful heating element and smaller boiler and yet another was to adopt the 'flow boiler' which was now being used in the domestic filter machines. This certainly meant that coffee made with freshly heated water was used in the office machines. It also provided for many young people in England their first introduction to practical and trouble-free coffee making.

The early experience of manufacturers with stainless-steel filter machines and the improvements in reliability and design in elements and thermostats gave them the confidence to introduce domestic filter machines in plastic cases. One of the first of these to be seen in Europe in the 1960s was the little Philips machine which used as its power source a heating element in the base which not only forced the heated water up and over the coffee but also doubled as a hotplate. Many manufacturers both in Europe and America followed with either combined hotplate elements or flow boiler designs and they all benefited from the latest technology in plastics and glass production.

These new domestic filters were an era away in design from the early commercial machines, but it was only the new technology in electronics which made the new designs possible.

SIMPLE COFFEE-MAKERS

There have always been devices which would brew coffee successfully in small quantities without the aid of any mechanical aid apart from gravity. Most of them are some sort of filter machine and they are extremely suitable for making one or two cups of coffee in the kitchen or any informal surroundings where the ceremony and appearance of more complicated coffee makers is not important. They are almost as simple to use as opening a tin or jar of instant coffee and to many people infinitely preferable.

One of the oldest individual forms of coffee filter is the metal cone with a rim which sits on the cup. It does not need a filter paper since it has holes or slits to strain the coffee and it usually has a lid attached. It was intended to be used with a coffee pot rather than a cup because the bottom part of the cone was several inches deep. It was very popular not only in Europe but also in the United States as the 'Phylax' and 'Private Estate' coffee makers.

The metal filters were very simple kitchen utensils, but they were transformed into something very much more attractive when they were made in ceramics. A lot of these appeared in about 1910 in Germany where they were

1

2

3

1 - French cone-shaped filter in tin plate with hinged lid. These simple filters fitted into the top of a coffee pot and have been around for more than a century. In America similar ones were sold as Phylax coffee makers.

2 - Pretty ceramic version of the simple cone filter from Hamburg, c. 1910. Courtesy Melitta Coffee Company.

3 - The Carlsbad or Bohemian coffee pot which had slits in its ceramic filter instead of holes. Courtesy Melitta Coffee Company.

4

5

4 - A silver-plated drip pot which sat on top of the coffee cup. Bramah Collection.

5 - Plunger pots in which hot water is poured onto the grounds and the plunger is pushed down to separate the grounds from the liquor. Old Italian and French metal pots on either side of a modern one in glass.
Bramah Collection.

6 - Manually operated pressure pot from the 1950s. The hot water in the upper chamber is forced through the coffee when the two "antennae" are pulled downwards like a sommelier's cork extractor.

7 - Left: A modern plastic version of the old French drip pot. Right: Coffee-maker which is a plastic stand with a filter funnel which can be moved up or down so that the coffee can drip into a cup or jug. The funnel has a permanent 'gold' filter.

mostly white with pretty painted flowers and there are modern ones still being manufactured today which, although perfectly practical for making coffee, are really intended as souvenirs.

The café version of the cone drip filter was more elaborate. It did not have the cone base but was a little metal can with a metal strainer in the bottom and it had a lid which doubles as a saucer to put the filter on when the water had passed through.

There was a time not very long ago when it was impossible not to encounter these all over continental Europe. Many English tourists can remember sitting in front of a cup, surmounted by a tiny filter pot brimming with hot water which filtered through the grounds so reluctantly that the resulting coffee was too cold to melt the lumps of sugar. Metal drip pots never commended themselves to the British, but there are modern versions in plastic which are much better at retaining the heat. There is a measured portion of ground coffee confined between two filter papers which make up the base and they take the idea of the teabag one stage further. They are the modern, disposable coffee pot and the ultimate in convenient, trouble-free ways of making an

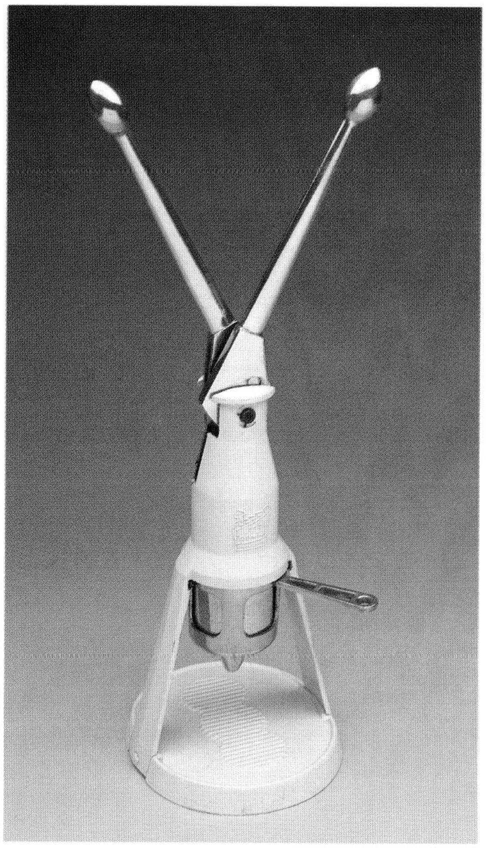

6

7

8/9 - Typical drip pot in white ceramic known as a "Carlsbad". This one is from the Carlsbad factory. It has a water spreader which fits on top of the coffee.

10 - Modern Melitta plastic filter funnel with filter paper which completely eliminates the problem of grounds escaping into the liquor. The modern plastic coffee jug retains heat better than glass, but a low power hotplate is often necessary.

8

9

11 - Teapot from the 1950s with an extra metal container and filter to convert it into a drip pot for making coffee.

12 - Coffilta "Hotpor". Pre-heated hot water is poured directly onto ground coffee in the funnel to filter into the jug. A hot-plate keeps the coffee at serving temperature.

10

11

12

13

13 - Modern disposable one-cup filter in plastic fitted with a measured portion of ground coffee between two filter papers. It combines cheapness and convenience with an attractive appearance. They are sold stacked and sealed in a sleeve like plastic cups. The plastic filter retains the heat well and they take all the uncertainty out of coffee making. Courtesy of SAS Ltd. Beerse Belgium.

individual cup of coffee. They are stacked in the same way as sleeves of disposable cups and can be used anywhere where there is a supply of boiling water. All that is necessary is to like the particular blend and strength of coffee.

The convenience of disposable filter papers designed to fit specific filter funnels has also produced a number of coffee makers which are really a light, toughened glass or plastic flask with a plastic funnel which is made to fit. It holds the grounds in a filter paper and the coffee is made simply by pouring boiling water on top. With a coffee suitable to this method, it is probably the simplest that can be devised while leaving the choice of coffee completely to the consumer.

The other major coffee maker that is included here since it does not have any source of heat and is basically a filter, is the plunger pot. Pots of this type, although often associated with the name Melia who was a German porcelain manufacturer, have been popular for a long time in Europe, and particularly German-speaking Europe. They were really a device for separating the grounds from the liquor after it was brewed rather than straining the water through a filter. The boiling water was poured onto the coffee grounds in the pot. The plunger, which was perforated with holes, was fitted on top and then pushed down, restraining the grounds and leaving the liquor clear. The classic Melia pot was a ceramic jar which retained the heat well, but it was a design which adapted happily to metal and then glass and clear plastic jars. It has certainly been around for a century and is the sort of design which never quite goes out of fashion but reappears every few years slightly changed to suit the current fashion.

CONTEMPORARY COFFEE-MAKERS

As electricity overtook gas as the most convenient source of domestic power, machines were developed to clean, wash and cook. The transition was gradual and until the start of the Second World War, electrical appliances were only within the reach of the more affluent families.

While washing machine and vacuum cleaner manufacturers introduced startling new ideas to a growing market, coffee machine makers were largely content to fit an electric element to a known and tried method of brewing. There was a good deal of sense to this. Nearly a century before, every possible internal arrangement of percolator and filter had been thoroughly explored and those which had survived had proved themselves acceptable and saleable.

The simple percolator and the pressure pot were particularly suitable to be adapted to use electricity. In fact they gained from it since they were no longer dependent on stoves and open fires and the modern thermostat meant that they could be safely left. The perennial problem of the self-extinguishing device which had added so much uncertainty to the coffee-makers heated by spirit lamps was solved at last. The simple, single-cycle percolator disappeared almost entirely and for a long time, the gentler action pumping percolator became the most popular type of electric coffee-maker, glamorised by its American associations.

Provided that its basic defect of boiling the liquor could be accepted at all, the pumping percolator seemed to have the overwhelming advantage that it could be left to perform its questionable work for twenty minutes or half-an-hour without danger of burning out the element or fusing all the electrical system in the house.

The pressure pot, which Rabaut had first introduced to London in 1822 and Caseneuve to Paris in 1824, was positively improved by being incorporated into a modern electric coffee maker. The spirit heater and valves were taken away and the ascending tube and coffee box were all contained in a nickel-plated or stainless steel case with a strong metal outlet tube to guide the liquor into a coffee pot. They were very much safer. It was no longer necessary to understand the elements of physics and the way to work steam engines, only how to fill a pot and turn a switch. Pressure pots became very popular in the 1930s and are still being made today.

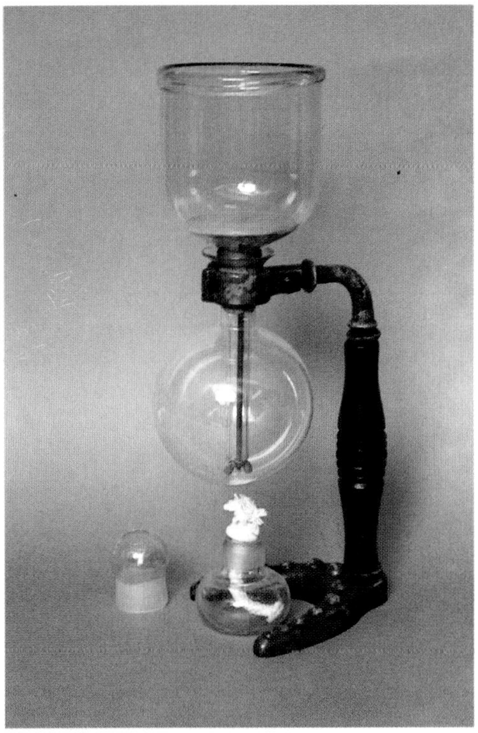

1

2

3

In 1946, after the war, a great deal of Europe had to be rebuilt and modernised. With modernisation came new ideas. A lot of Europeans had been made aware by the American troops of American tastes in coffee, but a great number of American troops had learnt about European coffee making. New materials and new technologies were about to become available for peacetime uses. An interval of nearly ten years had passed and a new generation of tourists was ready to discover other countries and other customs.

After a period of being overpowered by the energy and economic superiority of the visitors from the United States, Europeans decided that they did not like coffee from the pumping percolator. They were able to assert this with greater confidence because they had the new espresso machines which were replacing the older café sets in the continental cafés and bringing a whole new culture into the United Kingdom. Even Americans became converted to 'coffee without boiling' and it began to be noticed that the electric coffee-makers, although clean, shining and safe, had basic defects in the way that they treated coffee.

4

5

1 - The classic Cona machine. Courtesy of the Cona Company.

2 - An Italian electric pressure pot pupular throughout Europe. Courtesy Ursula Becker Collection, Cologne.

3 - Italian pressure pot from about 1946 patented by Robbiati as the "Atomic" in Milan. Also marketed by A & M. G Sassoon in London.

4 - Italian 'Utentra' electric pressure pot. 1950s. Bramah Collection.

5 - 'Aremator' ceramic percolator made in Germany in about 1950. There were no metal parts except for the element. The coffee container had slits in the base to form a filter and the percolator tube had marks to measure the number of cups. Courtesy Ursula Becker Collection, Cologne.

6

7

8

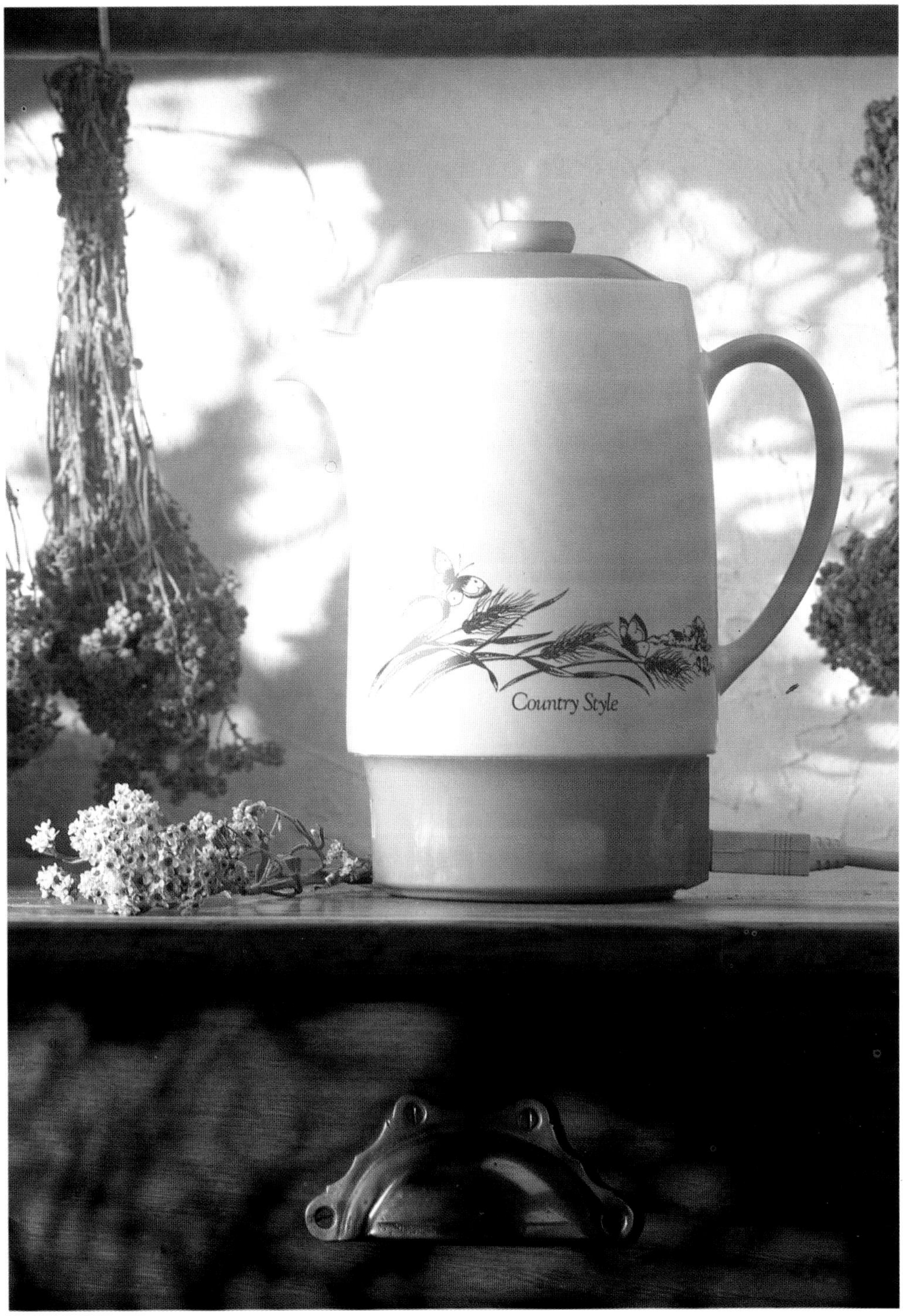

9

6 - The French 'Supermoka' which dispensed the liquor automatically into a pot. Bramah Collection.

7 - Percolator with milk-heater which has been in use for twenty years. Machines of this kind can make from ten to forty cups. Courtesy Arnold Gould Trading Company.

8 - 'Moulinex' Filter. Courtesy Moulinex Ltd.

9 - Russell Hobbs ceramic percolator of the 1960s. Courtesy of Russell Hobbs.

Pumping percolators, as has been said already, boiled the liquor and ruined the flavour. Modern pressure pots did not boil the brewed liquor, but because the pressure raised the temperature of the boiling water above normal boiling point, they pressure-cooked the grounds as the water passed through to give a very high extraction from the coffee. Pressure machines with a tube outlet are still popular, nevertheless, because they produce a strong brew which many people prefer.

In Italy, the days of the "napoletana" and "milanese" were numbered. Companies which had begun to manufacture modern coffee-makers before 1939, but whose development had to await the end of the Second World War, expanded rapidly in the favourable market conditions of the 1950s. Among these was Bialetti which enjoyed increasing success. While every new model which appeared before the public always had something extra to offer in design or technical improvement, Bialetti added an extra dimension to its publicity which recognised the growing sophistication of the public.

The company realised, as modern manufacturers must, that the mysteries of technology are no longer of paramount importance to the customer who expects them as a matter of course. Coffee-makers sell on the aesthetic appeal of the style, the durability of the finish and the assurance that operating them will present no problem. Bialetti stamped on their new models the figure of a little man with a moustache as their guarantee of high performance, a fairy godfather who would ensure that nothing could go wrong.

Filter machines had come a long way since their tentative beginnings at the end of the eighteenth century and the new improved pressure machines had also in their turn become a classic.

The Gaggia espresso machines in the coffee bars inspired several domestic versions of the espresso principle which adapted well to a small model. Electricity heated the water and a single spring-powered piston transferred it at will through the coffee. Coffee drinkers had what they

10

11

12

thought they had always wanted, a way of making a cup of fresh, individually-brewed coffee. Long acquaintance with the domestic espresso machines usually brought disillusion. It was a nuisance to have to knock out the grounds after making each cup of coffee. The cups were very small and the traditional taste in Germany and northern Europe favoured a less strong and a lower roasted coffee.

These traditional tastes were still served by the Cona machines with their heat-resistant flasks. These were essentially the same as the French cafetières of a hundred years before except that they had an electric heat source. Reliable, replaceable and looking modern in every age that they had reappeared in, glass flasks had a faithful following, particularly now that electrically-heated hotplates had extended their range so that it was less often necessary to wait for twenty minutes while a fresh batch of coffee was put through the cycle. However, new plastics, new electronics and years of experiments and testing by the catering trade had brought the domestic filter machine to the point where it was practicable to launch it successfully upon the public.

10 - Modern revival of a 1950s coffee bar espresso machine with the curves, pipes, valves and sparkling chrome. A prototype made by Mike Stallion from components supplied by Rowenta. It is intended as a nostalgic contrast to the newer plastic models.

11 - Russell Hobbs Filter. Courtesy Russell Hobbs Ltd.

12 - The original Mr. Coffee automatic drip coffee-maker which was introduced in the United States in 1972 and quickly became the best-selling domestic model in America. In 1989 it was still the best-selling machine, selling more machines each year than the next two brands put together. Courtesy of Mr. Coffee Inc., Ohio.

The market leader was the American 'Mr. Coffee' which was launched in 1972 by North American Systems. Nickel,

13

aluminium and stainless-steel had been abandoned and clean, cream plastic was used with a heat-resistant jug printed with white flowers. Trouble-free food mixers and automatic ovens had conditioned the public to expect trouble-free coffee makers and the new filters were designed to provide it.

The original 'Mr. Coffee' had a heating element in the boiler at the top and fed boiling water into a filter funnel and filter paper containing the coffee, and from there to a flask on a hotplate. European filter machines put their element into a compartment at the back of the machine and a flow boiler heated the water and fed it up a tube and onto the coffee. Plastic cases were made in different colours. Switches, filter funnels, hotplates and jugs were

14

15

13/15 - Three coffee makers from the same company, Bialetti, showing that there is a place for the traditional and also for the latest style. The aluminium pot with the faceted sides has been popular so long that its 1930s appearance has become a major part of its charm. It is a pressure pot like the Parker steam fountain or Vienna Incomparable. The later design makes use of the latest metal and composition finishes. It is intended to be high fashion aimed at a market where only the very latest will do.

refined. The mechanisms were varied and perfected but the people who used them did not need to understand them any more. Anybody who could press a switch could now expect to get a good cup of coffee.

As the world becomes a single market, customs which were once confined to a family group of countries have become completely international. The great tea-drinking nations of China and Japan have discovered coffee and Japanese technology has not been slow to develop a range of machines to exploit it.

If there is any conclusion to be drawn from this book it is that no method of making coffee ever dies. Complications and improvements come but do not entirely go. The history of

16

16 - The typically Western design belies the oriental origins of this Japanese coffee filter. Toshiba's "filtermill" is aimed both at an export market and also an increasing interest in coffee in the traditional land of green tea.

coffee-makers and machines is not so much a carousel as a spiral staircase. We come round again to the same place but at a higher point: something has been added, an improved technology, a more modern design. There has always been a new twist to the old story, and probably there always will be.

BIBLIOGRAPHY

William H. Ukers, M.A., All About Coffee (The Tea & Coffee Trade Journal, New York, 1922)

Aytoun Ellis, The Penny Universities. A History of the Coffee Houses (Secker & Warburg, London, 1956)

A.E. Haarer, Modern Coffee Production (Leonard Hill (Books) Ltd., London, 1958)

Frederick Bradbury, History of Old Sheffield Plate (J.W. Northend Ltd., Sheffield, 1968)

Edward Robinson, The Early English Coffee House (The Dolphin Press, Christchurch, Hants., 1972)

Egon Viebahn, Bergisches Zinn (Dr. Wolfgang Schwarze Verlag, 1972)

Henry Sandon, Coffee Pots and Teapots For the Collector (John Bartholomew & Son Ltd., Edinburgh, 1973)

Jeol, David & Karl Schapira, The Book of Coffee & Tea (St. James Press, London, 1975)

Kenneth Davids, The Coffee Book (Whittet Books Ltd., Weybridge, Surrey, 1976)

Claudia Roden, Coffee (Faber & Faber, Middlesex, England, 1977)

Harry Rolnick, The Complete Book of Coffee (Melitta, 1982)

Kenneth Anderson, Coffees & Teas (Frederick Muller Ltd., London, 1982)

Bernhard Rothfos, Coffee Curiosa (Gordian-Max Rieck GmbH., Hamburg, 1986)

Philipps Jobin, Bernard Van Leckwyck, Le Café (Nathan, Paris, France, 1988)

INDEX

Page numbers in bold refer to illustrations